ALSO BY JAMES LORD

Stories of Youth

A Gift for Admiration

Some Remarkable Men

Making Memoirs

Six Exceptional Women

Picasso and Dora

Giacometti: A Biography

Giacometti Drawings

A Giacometti Portrait

PLAUSIBLE PORTRAITS OF

JAMES LORD

PLAUSIBLE PORTRAITS OF

JAMES LORD

WITH COMMENTARY BY THE MODEL

FARRAR, STRAUS AND GIROUX / NEW YORK

Farrar, Straus and Giroux
19 Union Square West, New York 10003

Distributed in Canada by Douglas & McIntyre Ltd.
Printed in the United States of America
First edition, 2003

Library of Congress Cataloging-in-Publication Data
Lord, James.
Plausible portraits of James Lord : with commentary by the model / James Lord.— 1st ed.
p. cm.
Includes index.
ISBN 0-374-28174-2 (hc. : alk. paper)
1. Lord, James—Portraits. 2. Portraits—Psychological aspects. 3. Portraits—History—20th century. 4. Portrait photography—Psychological aspects. I. Title.

N7628.L58 L67 2003
704.9'423—dc21

2002027855

Designed by Jonathan D. Lippincott

www.fsgbooks.com

1 2 3 4 5 6 7 8 9 10

CONTENTS

FOREWORD

What is a portrait? No element, certainly, essential to the continuity of human life. Assuming, however, the portrait to be a work of art, it possesses a durable existence all its own, not powered by muscles and blood, to be sure, but by a constitution which survives in reality and contributes to our limited lives a vivifying intimation of eternity. What more persuasive purpose can there be for human beings to create works of art than the yearning that these shall outlive them? And they do. Those fated to appreciate art find that it adds to experience a magically magnified dimension of vitality, within which one dwells somewhat as a single snowflake in a blizzard. Intimacy with art is therefore desperately personal. Amongst those masterpieces which have survived the myriad madnesses of mankind, the intemperance of nature, and the wastage of the millennia, the greatest are the most solitary. The Parthenon, Bach's B-Minor Mass, Keats's odes, and Cézanne's apples all bid us to consider them with a selfless concentration that acknowledges the universal solitude of things, and then—but only then—they can respond with their sublime revelation that the solitude of men and of things are one and the same, whereupon a painted apple, a phrase of music, a ruined temple, a poem may assume the configuration and identity of the cosmos. Such is the frail human compulsion to search for meaning beyond reason. What incomprehensible creatures are we, for whom the breath of life is sung or painted or written or built of stone! And yet we know that our species alone can confront and overcome its physical, intellectual, and historical limitations by mindful yielding to the truth of art.

A portrait, thus, even before it begins to represent its aesthetic, social, and personal raison d'être, bears a weighty metaphysical burden by virtue of being a creation brought into existence from nothingness, the product, in short, of a transcendent act. That this smacks of something akin to sacrilege is self-evident and may presently bring about the loss of artistic creation in favor of technological invention. Acts of scientific penetration, after all, have brought to mankind's awareness splendid revelations, albeit of phenomena already extant, though unknown, and thus are not products of pure creativity but practical discoveries in a realm of which the future is in fact an incomprehensible past. The potential for controversy, not to mention misunderstanding, seems infinite. Who, for example, is to determine with absolute assurance whether Heisenberg's uncertainty principle is as great, beautiful, and moving an expression of human attainment as Beethoven's Ninth Symphony? Luckily it is neither my prerogative nor my presumption to have, much less to advance, an opinion. Looking backward, in any case, provides a far wealthier prospect for meditation upon the paradox in human experience which brought forth portraits.

In ancient Egypt a sculptor was known as "one who keeps alive," which he did principally by modeling in diverse materials innumerable votive and funerary objects needed to depict the multitude of living things, some of them, incidentally, human, essential to the arcane rites of Egyptian religion. Almost none of these sculptures attempted to faithfully represent an individual physiognomy, though the specific features of certain royal personages, especially during the short Amarna period, are recognizable. In Mesopotamia as well as Egypt, artistic work was ruled so strictly by convention that purposeful likenesses of living persons were viewed with indifference, whereas symbolic, traditional effigies were countless and often monumental. Oddly enough, given the supreme skills of Greek painters and sculptors, portraiture per se seems not to have stirred their ambitions, and it was only as the Hellenistic world of Alexander began to merge with the Roman republic that portraiture as we recognize it today became prevalent. The most striking and lifelike portraits of this early period are the famous funerary paintings found in profusion beneath the sands in a northwestern corner of Egypt called Faiyum. From the earliest times portraits were widely believed to confer access to immortality, and the Faiyum portraits, painted with unsparing exactitude and striking technical virtuosity, were made—probably during the model's lifetime—to adorn his mummy with his effigy as a passport, so to speak, for the voyage into the hereafter. These very early and specific portraits were therefore free from any taint of vanity or infection of flattery. To see their equals in freedom of representation it would be necessary to wait a thousand years. Republican and Imperial Rome left innumerable portrait sculptures, of course, but these are not objective, reliable likenesses, as sculptors were compelled to please wealthy or imperial clients, while stone, moreover, does not lend itself with such plastic ease to figurative representation as paint or even pencil and paper. Caesar, Augustus, Caligula, and Hadrian as well as numerous other rulers, senators, men, women, and children of the upper classes are nonetheless familiar faces in the world's great museums and private collections, but their features have lost to vandalism, restoration, and time the lifelike likeness so striking in the portraits from Faiyum.

And yet these conventional Roman stones and occasional bronzes express extravagant vainglory, smug self-satisfaction, pensive serenity, handsome innocence, vicious cruelty, and, above all, imperturbable indifference to the inherent dignity of an individual human life. Games of death, indeed, were a thrilling public entertainment throughout the Roman world until the Western empire was annihilated in the fifth century. The barbaric Visigoths, Huns, and well-named Vandals cared nothing for portraits, portraiture, or the glories of historical civilization and destroyed or neglected what they could not be bothered to plunder, whereupon all of Europe sank into the heartless gloom of the Middle Ages, saved from utter oblivion only by the faint but defiant glimmer of graven gold and religious faith.

And, ironically, it was the power and the glory of the church that little by little raised from obscurity the art and the act of portraiture, though had the contemporary popes ever suspected what human frailties and brazen breaches of piety would proceed from this creativity they would surely have issued a bull to prevent it. But Their Holinesses were too preoccupied at the time by the Great Schism and by down-to-earth corruption within the papacy itself to be troubled about artistic matters. The men, beginning with Giotto, who painted magnificent frescoes and altarpieces to glorify Christian faith were presently paid to include in their symbolic religious scenes portraits of the donor and his family. Portraits of individuals inevitably followed, often of the worshipful donors themselves as strictly secular human beings. Thereafter it was but a half-step to portraits of the popes themselves, their nephews, humbler prelates and prestigious noblemen, poets, and persons of worldly eminence, whose distinction nourished a hankering for glory and for the blessed bargain of immortality. The propriety and prestige of portraiture as an autonomous mode of artistic expression, thus, was assured by the beginning of the fifteenth century. The roster of artists who gladly devoted themselves to the portrait inspires not only awe but also an awareness that a spiritual ideal of man's relation to man and to the world, an ideal harking back nearly two thousand years, had been reborn. This, of course, was the emergence of the Renaissance. It would be vain to list the great masters whose works of portraiture, often depicting themselves, are as moving, mysterious, and profound as *The Adoration of the Lamb* or the ceiling of the Sistine Chapel. Surely, moreover, it is pertinent to point out that the most celebrated painting in all the world is a portrait, created by a man unique in the history of civilization.

Now, it is relevant to ask what is the meaning of a portrait, what the purpose, what the personal, aesthetic, sensuous value, what the revelation of human nature, what the significance of relations between artist and model, model and artist, and what the status of both and, indeed, of posterity itself as observers of a human creation, an image of humankind which happens to be a portrait but which even as such remains a reality apart.

A portrait is a pictorial or sculptural representation of a person and usually shows at least the face. It is unrelated to the photograph, which despite countless advocates to the contrary has nothing to do with the concept of art. And it is art, a creation of the human brain, eye, and hand, which brings to a portrait its broadest and deepest meaning. Art, to be sure, at its most mediocre, facile, and/or incompetent is nonetheless art, albeit bereft of ontological import. A shoddy commercial portrait still possesses a relation, however impoverished, to the supreme yearning for timeless identification with the enigmatic evolution of men and women on earth. Portraits of them show that they have lived. They will not do so indefinitely, of course, but their portraits may, even those few forgotten for centuries in foreign attics. And in this self-defeating quest for fragile but visible perpetuation dwells the irrational meaning of every portrait. Its purpose consequently is not only to defy biological inevitability but also to make a very sweeping and preposterously presumptuous metaphysical statement. The value in personal terms is almost infinitely variable, because it depends entirely upon the innate characters of the two individuals directly involved in its creation. Aesthetic quality, on the other hand, is by definition limitless because *it* depends on nothing other than the skill, the talent, and the perspicacity—the genius, in short—of the artist, who may make a masterpiece from the visage of a madman.

The sensuous distinction of a portrait, of any work or concept created by the human mind, is an evaluation of the capacity to find delight in the beauty or grandeur of a specific creation, and, as such, being perforce subjective, exists at the fickle mercy of the craze called taste. How ineluctably, then, do works of art and the circumstances of their appreciation, and most especially an assessment of portraits, reveal in terms of experienced time the changeless constituents of human nature. So the portrait paradox resides fundamentally in the mysterious relations between artist and model, model and artist, and the seeming identification with an image to which each mistakenly believes his conduct to have been essential. Certainly the portrait per se requires an artist, but the artist's accomplishment takes for granted a veracity inherent in art itself, which cannot exist without a suspension of doubt in regard to the principle of illusion. Thus, within the artist's hand lives the existential lie beneath a glorious truth which from nothingness can wring no more than a supposition, and therein, of course, dwells the marvelous fact of an artist's indispensable irrelevance. That so many have succumbed to the circumstantial evidence of the self-portrait testifies to the awe-inspiring frailty of spiritual endeavor. It can hardly be a coincidence, though, that the greatest artist of modern times (*not* the most famous) has bequeathed to us the largest number of great self-portraits. Genius does die, its works wither, fade, grow old, decay, and rejoin in oblivion the very idea of art, to which both artist and model have made sacrifices beyond their means. The model, to be sure, is no less important to the portrait than the artist, for it is he, or she, who provides to talent or to genius the opportunity to pursue a quest for the self by contributing to life's adventure a likeness destined—also!—to die. To surrender one's appearance to the transubstantiation of the creative act is, indeed, to take a step toward death by adding to the litter of civilization an object which presumes to better it by outliving mere history.

The hubris of the model, whether purposeful or not, goes even farther than the folly of the artist, for it supposes that the memory of mankind—notoriously fickle—may be led by art to take kindly to a ludicrous love for imaginative immortality. This senseless craving for any sort of survival beyond life's normal conclusion unites artist and model in a paradoxical semblance of reality which is the raison d'être sine qua non of a portrait. In appearance like a human being, it is not a living thing at all, only an image: one, however, which at its best can offer to mankind a delusive but vivifying sense of human truth. A model contemplating his likeness will see himself peering through the scrim of art; imprisoned within the portrait, he gazes outward in the hope of getting out, so to speak, alive. But he never will, having relinquished his identity to the whim of the artist, who is also a prisoner of the creation, for as his hand has worked to capture the presence of the model a vital part of the substance of his own life has flowed away from him forever into his work. Only the portrait ultimately remains: captivating, enigmatic, present, even touchable, but at the same time remote and unfeeling. It may reveal something of the social, financial, intellectual, emotional condition of the model, yes, also the psychological attitudes, prejudices, and ambitions of the artist, combining narrative with portraiture and displaying a relative depth of understanding of human nature, but in the end it bids us to see, if we can, our own reality through the unreal eyes of an artifice which embodies via the inexplicable use of nonhuman materials the most profound and thrilling aspects of a civilization that we are at a loss to explain.

In awe we can only contemplate the images of men and women who once lived and now "survive" through the mysterious medium of genius, leading one into one's self through the eyes of individuals long since dead. Of the millions of portraits painted, sculpted, carved, engraved, embroidered, or made of next to nothing, only a meager handful by the greatest of artists possess the power, beauty, and perception essential to profound appreciation and explication. The rest perish, if not physically, then spiritually and aesthetically, having in fact never really lived, while through the great museums of the world herds of blind but innocent tourists are unprofitably paraded before portraits created by the likes of Leonardo, Titian, Velázquez, and Cézanne. Vision, unfortunately, like knowledge, comes at a cost that few are in any position to pay.

When I was four or five, my dog, a brown spaniel, was run over and killed by a car. It was my first encounter with death, and at that age most children are as curious about the mystery of dying as they are about the mystery of birth. The truth about the incomprehensible transition from being to nothingness will haunt them till the final instant of consciousness, and countless human beings practice all sorts of symbolic acts in the hope of thwarting that inevitable instant. Posing for a portrait is one of these. Perhaps children are unlikely to dwell very much upon the imminence of death, since the secret of childhood is that life goes on forever, but they will soon enough be pinched by the vise of impending mortality. And this, after all, may turn out to work the very trick that imagination needs in order to counteract utter nonentity. Youth adores audacity.

I made myself at home in museums. I made, indeed, a museum of my home, my bedroom, that is, in the house of my parents—rather to their dismay—and the dormitory rooms—earning the scorn of my classmates—of the boarding schools and the university I attended. My walls were cluttered with fifth-rate watercolors and etchings culled from parental attics and shoddy thrift shops. Poor as they were, however, they were nonetheless works of art, related only by infinite light years, but related all the same, to the masterpieces I revered at the Metropolitan and the Frick, some of which, as a matter of fact, merged sensual attraction with sensuous appreciation. Titian's *Portrait of a Man in a Red Cap* at the Frick, for example, or the Met's copy of Polykleitos's *Diadoumenos*. By this time I was obviously aware that the emotions aroused by works of art were not solely aesthetic but to an appreciable degree partook of pragmatic desires induced by the looks and likenesses of beautiful young men. This awareness, of course, was no momentous discovery. Socrates, after all, had made it congenially clear—too clear, in fact, to suit many of his fellow Athenians—that the sensuous and the sensual are naturally interactive. But at age seventeen such insight came as a momentous self-discovery, easing the malaise of knowledge less tolerable in 1939. Much as I loved the images with which I became intimate in museums, it did not yet occur to me that they proposed to deal in the lovely illusion of deathless duration, or, indeed, that being portraits, they were also tokens of surrender.

In the rainy October of 1944 I learned as a soldier how absolutely and immutably mortal the dead can appear. Corpses never return a look of longing. Falling in love with the fantasy of immortality seems the least one can do when daily death falls like the rain and no works of art are available for making peace with war. Titian, not to mention Polykleitos, being even deader than the dead who populated my dreams, I pondered the possibility of coming face-to-face with a substitute genius, and the obvious person was Picasso. In 1939 in New York I had seen a large exhibition of his paintings at the Museum of Modern Art and became enamored of the sad-faced but beautiful young men, brooding acrobats, wistful dogs, and monkeys of the Blue and Rose periods.

Five years later, relieved from duty at the front, I found myself in Paris and made my way to Picasso's doorstep. I've never been able to guess why he repeatedly accepted with amiable tolerance not only my visits but also my requests. This was not invariably his habit. Perhaps he understood how vulnerable I was even then to the apparent but cryptic and symbolic appeal of portraiture. Having executed hundreds, if not thousands, of portraits, including many of himself, and some of them grim images of torment and distortion, he surely realized that a portrait can make a man question his reality. And a portrait of myself was simply the unconscionable thing I had the supreme temerity to ask him to create. He promptly did a drawing. I didn't much like it, so a few months later I asked him to make another, which he willingly did, a superb example of faultless draftsmanship and a striking likeness, executed in less than five minutes. A masterpiece, declared his secretary. Maybe. But who can say with everlasting authority just what that is? About Picasso's power and genius, at all events, there can be no question. Like talismans of something I could not comprehend, I carried his drawings with me from place to place until the end of the war.

Perhaps Picasso's generosity, of which I immodestly made no secret, prompted other artists to portray me. Quite a few throughout the decades have proposed to do so, which may not be entirely surprising, as I have always sought out the company of artists rather than authors. I willingly and patiently sat for them, and all my artist friends have been as generous with their works as Picasso was. That's why I possess so many likenesses of myself. To be fair, I may say that I, too, have been as generous as I could, making free not only with gifts but also with admiring articles and appreciative prefaces written for exhibition catalogues, of which I've composed about as many as the portraits I possess. To pose for the pencils or paintbrushes of artists was not precisely my profession, or even vocation, but it did become an avocation from which a singular satisfaction was forthcoming: a sense that I was actually participating in the transcendental process from which civilization is formed, a sense, moreover, that I have never known when doing what I'm doing now and have industriously done for more than half a century: writing. Maybe this signifies that what's visual is more meaningful to me than what's verbal. To write is nonetheless the indispensable nourishment of my continuity. The portraits, having been finished, framed, hung, stored, given away, sold, or lost, disclose nothing more important about me as an individual than my perishable features can do. The writings, on the other hand, make an earnest issue of candid disclosure of the character and temperament of the person behind the pen. And yet the sheer quantity of portraits of myself hanging on the walls of my apartment, twenty-three by careful count, must impress many as a brash display of vanity and smug conceit concerning the comeliness of my countenance, and also an all-too-visible disclosure of pride in having secured the attention of so many artists. A silly fact, however, is that when young I regretfully believed myself to be physically quite plain, if not actually ugly, and never realized until age had made me plain, though not actually ugly, that at twenty-five or thirty I'd been believably close to handsome. So today I contemplate with wistful empathy the attractive likenesses of a youth imbued with life long, long ago by Picasso or Dora. As for the pride of possession, yes, it exists, but it's a secret dark as death itself. Vanity, conceit, pride, all are pernicious tricksters to be shunned like fatal maladies.

Portraits undeniably have a lot to offer, but really and truly they demand a great deal more. What they most bestow, even when works of modest accomplishment, is the life-enhancing sense of having participated, however briefly and negligibly, in the only human doings that ennoble life on earth: the growth of civilization. This, of course, contributes a lovely feeling of responsibility. A portrait drawing by Picasso or Giacometti provides the perfectly absurd but delightful promise of living on indefinitely in the presence of one's self even when the quest for the self seems triumphantly to have been terminated. The triumph, of course, dwells in the illusion which the portrait itself lives by, and the quest succeeds insofar as it brings to a happy end the siege of the future, wherein lies the likeness of a man long since nameless. That's not such a bad eventuality to look forward to, and all those portraits say so.

But they are treacherous, too, those portraits. The price of their promise is highly disproportionate to the means of one who is not himself insightfully creative, rich beyond measure, that is, in the resources of surmise, and the demand for settlement is unending, till the wonderful terminus is a thing of the past. A poet I knew, who drew my portrait, incidentally, oftentimes remarked that if one searchingly scrutinizes one's image in the mirror, one sees the face of death. To stare at one's portraits can provoke a similar experience, but the mirror image, daring disclosure of the self, perishes, whereas the portraits are supposed to defy the fatal caprice of time. When the model, if a man, looks at his portrait, he sees a man, and if he is a man who loves men (as I am), then the countenance gazing back at him may easily resemble the love of his life. So he is face-to-face with the bottomless deeps of Narcissus, in which the vision of the self is an enticement to see—or is it to seek?—self-obliteration.

What more can I say? The portraits are there. They speak of a self who presumes, thanks to them, to see someone whose lifelong endeavor has been to be visible, to be legible, to be credible. The reward of so much effort, naturally enough, will be to never know whether it was all worthwhile, after all, after the artist's scrutiny, after the model's patience, after the portrait's survival, if someone should say, "The image is not the truth, not what it seems, not at all."

To gather reproductions of many of the portraits of myself, to write about them and about portraiture as an essence, so to speak, was not my initiative. It came as an intriguing proposal from my publisher and friend Roger Straus, who deserves heartfelt thanks offered in the hope that his expectation will seem in the end to have brought forth a little meaning. The portraits, to be sure, are there, and I have chosen to describe this collection of them as *plausible* because by its very nature a portrait, while possessing its own truth, is at the same time possessed by uncertainty as to the inherent credibility of what it presumes to represent. A portrait of a person is not, in short, a person. It is, at its best, a man-made thing which generates a vital sense of life without being actually alive. Thus, it defies the expectation of death, challenging human eyes to perceive in their own depths an enduring and emancipating reality.

The Delphic maxim "Know Thyself" can understandably be interpreted as "Look at Thyself," which naturally means "See Thyself." A portrait strives for such vision. As awareness, amoeba-like, divides in order to survive itself, the "other" self watching within ourselves is simply our death. One attains realistic self-knowledge via the ever-present perception of mortality. Such awareness is not only the essence of self-knowledge; it is also the key to art. A conclusive reality, this final, fatal conclusion exists between the artist and his model and the portrait to which they have both wantonly offered up more than they could afford to. And, indeed, as the model for many portraits, this selfsame conclusion has always hovered on before me toward a guiding vision of the future. No doubt it's done so in its own sly way ever since that day when we buried my little dog under the blue spruce in my parents' garden.

PLAUSIBLE PORTRAITS OF

JAMES LORD

PICASSO

Pablo Picasso was the preeminent portraitist of his period. In terms merely of quantity he was probably the preeminent portraitist of all time. And from the first, the features he most consistently commanded his talent to portray were his own. Already well before the age of twenty he had produced self-portraits inscribed, "I, the King." His passionate infatuation with self-representation knew no boundary, and over the coming three-quarters of a century thousands of images of himself in various guises spilled spontaneously from his fingertips. Even when he was portraying his wives, mistresses, children, friends, and casual passersby, he usually did so in such a manner that they were recognizable initially as Picassos and almost incidentally as individuals. Still, he could create arresting likenesses when he chose to. Indeed, it may almost have seemed that when he chose to he could create almost anything. In fact, he was sometimes heard to exclaim, "I'm God! I'm God!" This was even more exalting than to be king, and self-portraits were certainly to be viewed as objects entitled to devout veneration as the artist came closer and closer to the ultimate desecration of the model.

His hubris, however, did not vouchsafe the immortal doom of a tragic hero. He was too frightened by death to live on as a mythic figure. For all the illusory glory of his own lifetime, he had made so extravagant an outlay that even the fortune of the wealthiest artist in history could defray not a tithe of a tithe. Immense amounts of money have been paid for a Picasso self-portrait, but there precisely is the pitiless paradox. About the man's genius there is no question, and yet his commitment to the timeless truth of art was never sufficiently selfless to beget an artist able to further art's inherent capacity to become the redeeming element in human experience. This is not to imply that Picasso added little to the spiritual adventure of a direly troubled century. He added much. He added astonishing works of art, as to which, however, an uncertain future has still to make enduring assessments. He added an insatiable, almost maniacal and abject hunger for fame, leading to such a craven failure of integrity as fatefully falls upon a man—formerly the outspoken hero of creative freedom—prepared to support and praise without a murmur of remorse during the final third of his long lifetime a regime never surpassed for obscene evil: the Soviet Union. He added, when far too much has already been said, when what has been done has parlously been overdone, contradicted, exaggerated, and made meretricious, he added in a word, Picasso.

The quest for the self secreted behind that name played upon an imperious disposition to invent rather than to discern the unique and enigmatic human who gazes inscrutably back from behind those famous eyes so repeatedly portrayed as Picasso, Plato, Praxiteles, Bacchus, and Adonis, the philosopher, the clown, minotaur and toreador, harlequin, painter, poet, lover, juggler of beauty and ugliness, a man of whom everyone has heard but nobody knows, cre-

Pour James Lord

Picasso

PARIS 7 D. 44

ative daredevil who plays metaphysical tricks on naïve mankind, leaving in his wake works of art that do—or do they?—suspend all doubt in regard to the principle of illusion. Doubt, indeed, was Picasso's principal plaything, because he, all alone in his omniscient absoluteness, put an end to five hundred years of lovely confidence in the redeeming ideal of art as the lifeblood of the whole human community. Overnight the quest for the self could successfully be completed by the simple assertion, "I do, therefore I am." No cerebral activity was required. The offspring of those who had been scurrilous about van Gogh now crowded forward to consecrate excrement alongside nothingness in the pantheon of creative plenitude. Picasso is reputed to have remarked that he could draw as well as Raphael. Even as a bon mot it was no good. He could convincingly imitate Ingres if he felt like it. He could even sometimes impart to a tangle of lines the quick of life. He was amazing. But in and of and for and by himself he allowed his genius to use him in order to substantiate the dehumanization of the very ground upon which he had chosen to stake his own humanity and its otherworldly perpetuation. He was too sly not to know this, and the knowledge is pathetically self-evident in the pitiful self-portraits of the artist's final years. He was terrified of dying, having been too callous during his lifetime to envision the beauty of oblivion. Where in his *Inferno* Dante would have placed Picasso is a matter for tantalizing, somber, and lamentable conjecture.

Why today I take the liberty of articulating notions so long ago left idle is probably a simple surrender to the temptation of having a final fling with half a century's cumulative but supererogatory musings, which, of course, have everything to do with the possession, the pertinence, and the power of portraits, their maker and their model.

Of all such intimations, to be sure, I had not the slightest inkling in war-worn Paris in the month of December 1944, when I braced my brashness at the pinpoint of Picasso's doorbell. As to the durable changes in my life brought about by pressing it, I have quite sufficiently described them elsewhere, albeit without dwelling very much on the issue of portraiture per se, though the two drawings made of me by Picasso are by no means unmentioned. The treacherous seductiveness of a portrait had never before tempted my introspective vulnerability. To be sure in that long-ago, grisly autumn I had lived with the propinquity of death as never before or after. My own transformation into a corpse did not at the time seem likely, of course, because soldiers take their personal survival for granted. Besides, I was seldom in any danger. Dying, however, was very much on my mind, in my dreams and before my eyes, a single visit to a field hospital scarring one's visual remembrance more than enough to last a lifetime. But I looked for forgetfulness, too, in the belief that art could confer the only kind of immortality worth living for. Rembrandt, Beethoven, Balzac. Oh, I scanned the heavens, didn't I? And yet it's true, it's absolutely true I had no idea what my mind was doing, but it did believe in the grand hypothesis of greatness if I could but approach it, see it for myself, touch it, even possess the proof. Yes, my outrageous desire was merely to amount to more than James Lord could ever hope to, foolish boy. The really redeeming geniuses, however, were inconveniently immortal already. Nevertheless there was one who certifiably did live and create in the very land where worldwide insanity had sent me. So there *was* some existential cause concealed within the purpose, not to mention the propriety, of pressing Picasso's doorbell.

The first portrait which at my request he, or anyone else, for that matter, ever made of me was drawn during lunch in a restaurant called Le Catalan several days after the fateful tinkle of the bell. Genius is wont to fight shy of conquests that are too easy. To capture a likeness is one thing, to accept its surrender is very definitely another. I had made the acquaintance of a great artist, the most famous and emblematic of his era, and been given a portrait of myself from his hand, tangible proof—was it not?—that my person had commanded the scrutiny of a genius. Such consummation, I realized, comes to very few, and so I might naturally have assumed that in this domain of craving I had nothing further to desire, that my quest for vision into the self had gloriously been consummated. But no, this was only the beginning.

To start with, Picasso's portrait was a piercing disappointment. The secret self had evidently—and blindly—foreseen something altogether more comprehensive. In my diary I described the drawing as "A quick little sketch dashed off during lunch." That it happened to be a Picasso did not appear to provide what was wanted in the realm of revelation. The artist's attention and creative faculties clearly had not been engaged very deeply either by his model or by his drawing while I sat before him in the restaurant. I saw in my portrait evidence principally of haste and indifference—its inadequacy, not my own. The rendering of the GI-cut hair, the ear, the body, eye, and eyebrow, to be sure, is perfunctory. Not so the profile, however, which is aquiver, especially the mouth, vivid with feeling. And I didn't possess the insight to see what, in fact, I had been searching for. As a likeness, it's true, the portrait lacks much resemblance to the model. However, on the evidence of his drawing, Picasso appears to have glimpsed in me something similar to my own sentimental view of his Blue Period pictures of wistful harlequins and romantic acrobats, several of whom I'd fallen in love with five years before. The pensive, slightly melancholy, ambiguous aspect of my profile, and in particular the physically awkward but aesthetically effective depiction of the left shoulder hunched upward before the chin, seemed designed to compose an image imbued by the same narcissistic pathos I had thought to discern in Picasso's youthful art as a reflection of my adolescent self-indulgence and sensual desperation. Perhaps it's just as well that I didn't yet perceive what pursuit had led me to the rue des Grands-Augustins or suspect what wizardry enabled Picasso to see what I really wanted and give it to me by making a portrait so peculiarly like an evocation of *his* youth, not mine. In the catalogue of the 1939 exhibition whereby Picasso had first gotten me excited, I had underlined a statement by the artist: "A picture lives a life like a living creature, undergoing the changes imposed upon us by our life from day to day. This is natural enough, as the picture lives only through the man who is looking at it." He might have done well to add that the man who is looking is looked at. And I see now, fifty-eight years later, that that first portrait of me by Picasso makes a more visible demand upon the reality and vision of an old man than ever could have been expected of a youth.

The youth, meanwhile, having been relegated far from the battlefield to a bourgeois backwater in Brittany, engaged nonetheless in mental strife with his craving to be portrayed once again—and to

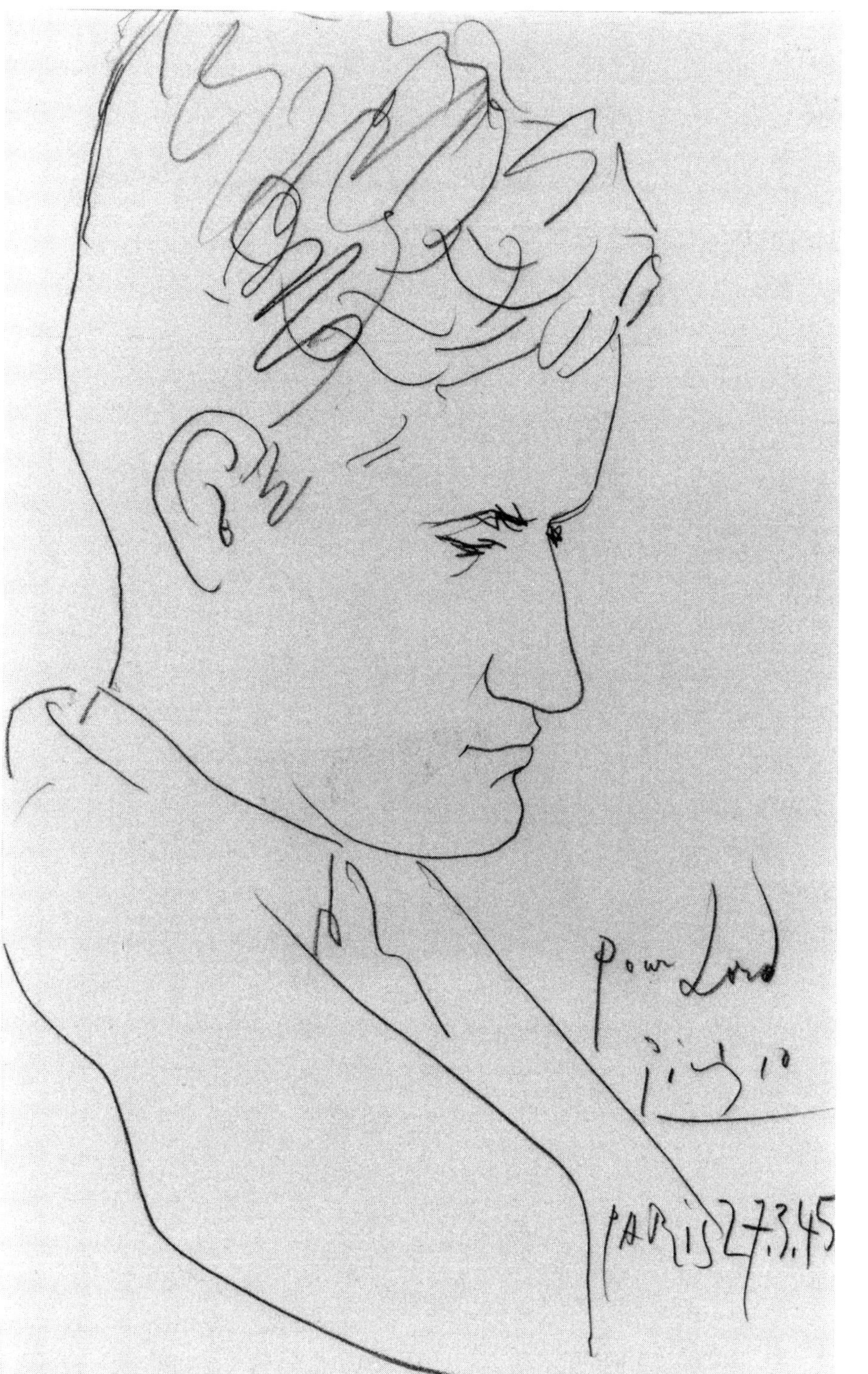
Pour Lord
Picasso
PARIS 27.3.45

his enduring satisfaction this time—by the baffling genius in Paris. Never for an instant did it occur to me that I might not chance to find myself once more in the presence of the indispensable artist. Nobody, I believe, having met him but once face-to-face, or knowing only his pictures, after all, could thereafter realistically foresee a time when Picasso might cease to loom over the perspective of things to come. As a prelude to dreams which I foreordained to be obedient, I puzzled and pondered about an infallible stratagem that might work like sunshine when in reply to my request Picasso would inevitably remark that his mastery of portraiture had been exercised to my advantage already. The only thinkable retort, I decided, would have to be misfortune. Unspeakable, ambiguous misfortune, its specific nature best left to the conjecture of an incomparable creator. This, of course, was before technology had begun to destroy the human imagination. To a man who lived in intimacy with the likes of Ovid and Aristophanes, the mere suggestion of misfortune could hardly be set aside as an effective cause. And it worked like magic, which it was, when eventually I asked him in front of three or four other men to draw once again my portrait. The conclusive inducement, I think, was nothing better than audacity, the stark, staring audacity of ingenuous awe.

This time there was to be no mistake about the size of the paper I had brought with me or the quality of the pencil. But there must have been a determining difference. Not in my physical appearance, I assume, but in an inner one. Several months had passed, during which, dismissed from Brittany, I had been involved in the frantic misery and accidental fates of prisoners and victims of war, and this had further afflicted what equanimity I had left. Who can say that this was visible? It so happened that at the very same time Picasso was working on an enormous painting which depicted a scene of atrocity, dead bodies in a ghastly heap, limbs disjointed, gruesome features twisted and contorted, a vision appallingly reminiscent of the prison camp so recently my place of "work," where weeping men clawed for a sip of water while others died of hunger in the mud. Neither I nor the artist referred to such aspects of civilization's dismemberment, but it existed.

He took the pencil, folded in half the sheet of paper, and told me to be seated on a chair some six feet away. My left profile was turned to him, so I couldn't tell how intently or how long he looked at me before beginning to draw. Not very long, because I quickly heard the pencil hissing on the paper, slowly at first, then faster, as if with a deliberate fury, while I hoped that this would go on forever, and then the whole business was done in less than five minutes. Picasso tossed the paper onto a nearby table. The witnesses crowded in front of me to see what had been drawn, and Sabartés, the artist's dour secretary, cried, "The latest masterpiece!" That exclamation embarrassed the model, but apparently no one else, least of all the artist. When I saw the drawing, I saw instantly—and at the time, perhaps, only—that it was what I had wanted. It was large, it looked like a likeness, and bore no resemblance whatever to the sketch dashed off in a restaurant sixteen weeks before.

I thanked the artist as he rolled up the drawing and slipped a rubber band around it. For all response he simply shrugged. When I went toward the door to leave, Picasso came with me and kissed me on both cheeks as I bent toward him to say goodbye. This certainly, was the beginning of an intimidating sort of friendship that was to last for a decade. I acquired a portfolio to protect the portrait, plus its predecessor, and carried them with me everywhere until the war was over, then back to America, then back to France, where I will remain as long as Paris survives. It has been with me always, though I gave the original ten years ago to the Picasso Museum here, a gesture that merits some musing, but to forestall complete privation I had an excellent facsimile made, very nearly indistinguishable from Picasso's own handiwork when framed under glass. So I have not lost my relation to a likeness.

A masterpiece is a work of whatever sort produced by an unquestioned master of the discipline entailed in its production. Whether or not Sabartés was right in so describing Picasso's second portrait of me I dare not say, but he was a lifelong connoisseur of the artist's work, and later, when we had become friendly, he once told me that he knew of no other portrait similar to mine in its bare linear volume and power limned with such sharp clarity of feeling conveyed as a kind of gleam refracted from my young sensibility, adding, moreover, that no other artist living—or dead?—could have produced an equivalent aesthetic vision of tenderness and determination. Oh, he added, he seemed to recall some vague resemblance to a sketch of the artist's son, Paulo, poring over a schoolbook, drawn about 1935 or 1936, but it was not nearly so stark and spirited. These were not his exact words, but they accurately enough convey the sense of what he said that summer afternoon and all I later recorded in my diary. Sabartés was a Romantic poet manqué, his life entirely dependent on Picasso's, who treated him with affectionate derision, and when he showed me with tremendous pride the portraits drawn of him by his employer, I sadly saw that none nearly deserved the description he himself had bestowed upon my own.

Of all the portraits made of me this second by Picasso is decidedly the one I have for fifty-seven years looked into most often and wherein I've sought to discern in a mysterious dissociation from the model the survival of a self within the image. There are, to be sure, other portraits executed years later that have concentrated my gaze no less significantly, but neither artist nor model were then the same, and the likenesses accordingly represent an altered quest. The Picasso remains uniquely what it is by being a sort of totem. There is a mystical relationship. Genius *can* command the perception of reality. To have portrayed so much so fast and by such infallible restraint was proof yet again, if any were needed, that Picasso's genius was the real thing. How often late at night I have stood in front of this drawing and been awed by the visible pulsation of its breath, knowing at the same time that concentrated observation acts upon the object being observed, and that simple, objective observation does not exist. Artistic awareness is inevitably a distortion, but this is not necessarily negative; it can become the instrument of momentous insights. Didn't Picasso, after all, say that a picture lives only through the man who is looking at it?

My portrait doesn't look at me. It gazes downward. How human and soulful are those seeming scribbles that actually see. Thus I stare up at myself, from my depths at a superficial, hypothetical, infinite likeness, and across universal space glimpse a multiplicity of ageless Lords on that irretrievable twenty-seventh day of March, 1945. What is wonderful, provocative, is the intense vitality of the line, how it moves without a motion to trace the absolutely valid profile, especially the quiver of the lips, asking if they quizzically smile or tremble with emotion. And the volume of the head, held steady by the tangle of the hair, is imagination made tangible once and for all. And yet the twenty-seventh of March, 1945, will exist again one day if the universe is indeed infinite, though neither Picasso nor his works nor even his memory, and certainly not James Lord, will be around to know it. But there in itself is the beauty of art, providing an opportunity to scrutinize one's self simultaneously from the innermost to the outermost reaches of one's likeness. If that be paradox—and it emphatically is if the laws of physics mean anything—then the opportunity is absolute perfection.

I never again aspired to be portrayed by Picasso.

CHAPOVAL

In the long, dusty room where Picasso's would-be visitors and sycophants were made to await the artist's whim, his walls held but a single painting, a tiny still life of a glass and lemon against a crimson background. There was also a small ink drawing of a crouching nude boy tacked up alongside it which I had from the first assumed to be a scrap from the long-ago Blue Period saved for sentimental reasons. One day I mentioned my assumption to Picasso, whereupon he immediately told me that not he but a young painter he admired was the draftsman. I was astonished that Picasso, who did not habitually advertise his admiration for other artists, would place beside a work of his own a drawing, however slight, by anybody else, especially someone younger than himself. The artist's name was Chapoval, and Picasso said I would do well to make his acquaintance, adding that this should not be difficult, since Chapoval frequently appeared unannounced at the rue des Grands-Augustins in the late morning, as I did. Within ten days or so we had met. This was in the early summer, the war in Europe by that time ended. From the first we got along famously. In fact, he immediately invited me to his home for lunch.

Chapoval and his wife, Marie, a good-looking and somewhat aristocratic blonde a bit older than he, lived in the small apartment-studio above an attractive tearoom-restaurant at the corner of the Boulevard Saint-Germain and the rue de Cluny, overlooking the museum gardens. I inferred that the wife had money, as the restaurant, linked to the apartment by an interior staircase, evidently belonged to her and there was ample food, proof of financial plenty in those days. Chapoval spoke with a slight accent. Physically imposing, with dark hair, piercing eyes, and a finely structured face, he was handsome, looked foreign, and, in fact, as I later learned, was by birth Russian. Born in one of Europe's most beautiful and culturally rich cities, Kiev, during the most brutal period of the anti-Bolshevik civil war, he was lucky to have had prescient and well-to-do parents who left the Ukraine when prudence told them to and moved to France, thereby avoiding the atrocities of the two most bloodthirsty tyrants of modern times. That they happened to be Jewish was taken for granted but never mentioned. His first name was Youla. He was twenty when World War II began. The ever-prudent Chapovals moved to Marseilles before the Nazis marched into Paris and divided France into "occupied" and "unoccupied" zones. Hopefully safe in the southern zone, Youla enrolled in the École des Beaux-Arts at Marseilles, where his precocious talent quickly made a mark. Anti-Semitism was popular in France, however, and even in the "unoccupied" zone Jews were soon being detained for "resettlement" in Eastern Europe. Youla stealthily made his way to Toulouse, hiding there and continuing to paint until peace delivered him from fear for his life but at the same time afflicted him forever with a searing awareness of the monstrous evil carried out by the

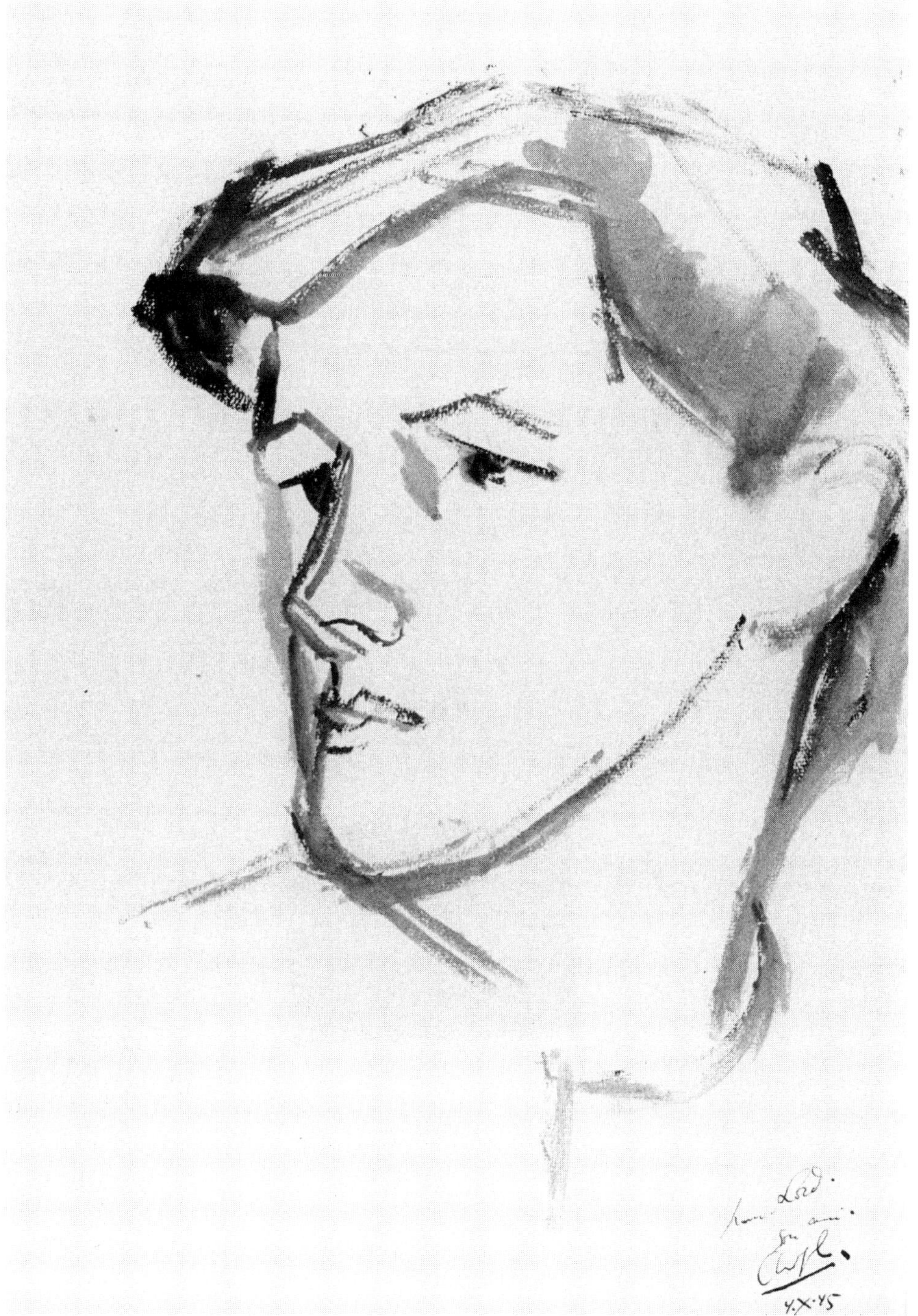
Lord.
4.X.45

Nazis against his people. I never learned what became of Youla's parents. He had a sister, but I saw her only once for five minutes. He was not given to reminiscence. Sometime in 1945, however, when information about Nazi abominations in Eastern Europe began to seep out, Youla painted a melancholy picture of a cheerless child held tenderly by a gaunt man wearing a Judaic hat, his eyes cast emptily in the direction of a nearby edifice with a black doorway and a high, bloodred chimney, a crematorium. How he became acquainted with Picasso I never knew. Maybe in the same way I did. They were made to be companionable, for Youla was unintimidated by genius or fame, while Picasso could agreeably grant esteem to a young fellow whose work owed a lot to the representational phase of synthetic cubism. Chapoval's painterly precocity was never in question. He was quick and powerful and original. Picasso later took to cultivating mediocre artists, but Youla was definitely not one of them.

During that lovely summer and autumn of 1945, I was very often with the Chapovals. Why Youla chose to make sketches of me I can't recall. He was more concerned then with the intricacy of still lifes than with the human figure. Maybe he was tempted because Picasso had already drawn me, that fact proving so frequently persuasive. In any event, I didn't ask him. Indeed, after Picasso I never again asked an artist to portray me. With the perverse exception of Balthus, portraits seemed to materialize because I was so often before the eyes of artists. Youla, in any case, was not concerned to create portraits as likenesses when in half an hour one October afternoon he painted two deft sketches in gouache. As the model I was but a coincidental pretext for the artist's release of primarily painterly impulses. Thus, the sensuous distinction of these two "portraits" is a revelation of Chapoval's instinctive compulsion to construct dynamic images resonant with the versatility of his brushwork rather than to discipline his skill in search of a model's physical resemblance. His accomplishment is assured by an intimate commitment to the veracity of human life truly illuminated by the most exalted feelings and deepest intuitions which art can create. One may regret that he was not prone to depict the human figure, but still lifes were clearly essential to him at this time for plumbing with intricate resourcefulness the depths of his pictorial idea. But then . . . there may have been incommunicable intuitions which made human representation personally oppressive.

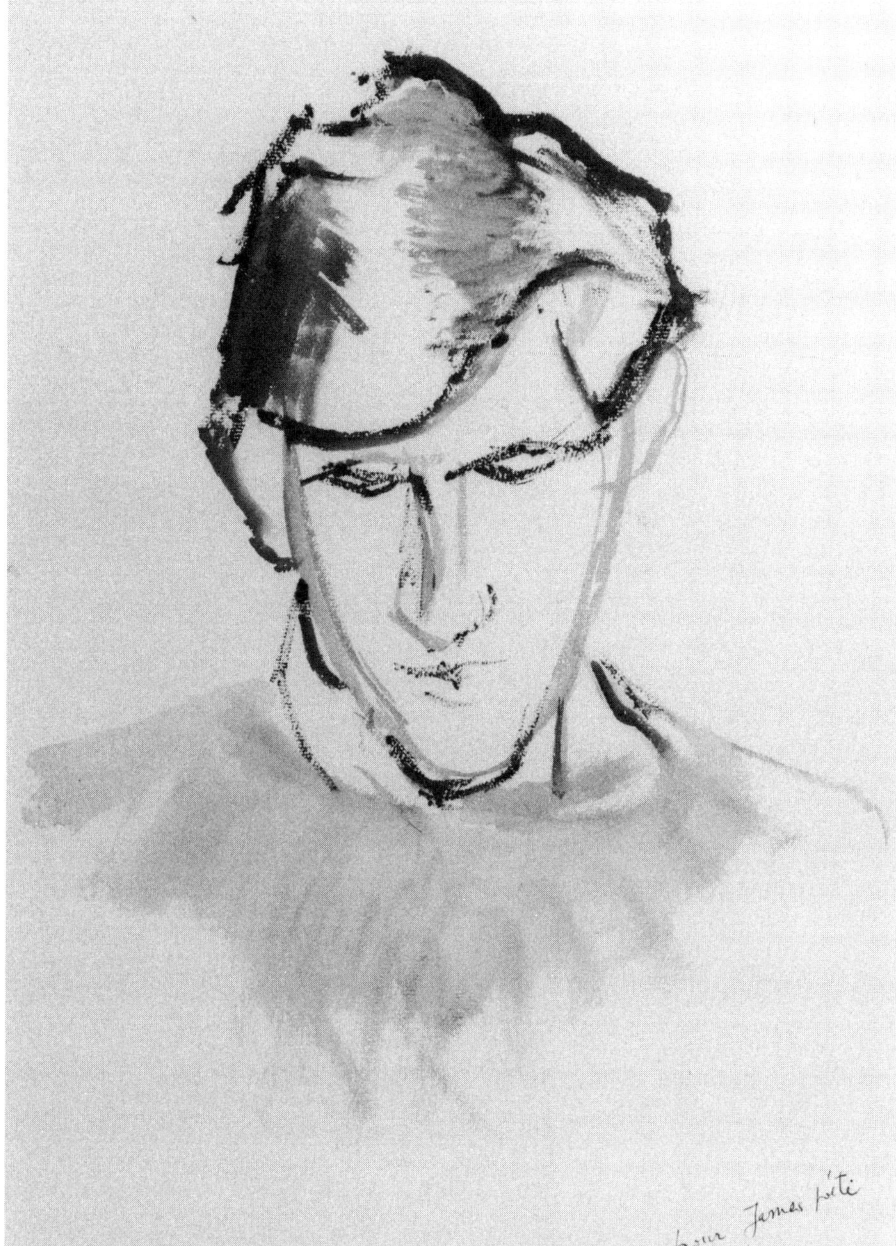
Pour James poète
4 X 45

GINDERTAEL

It was Gindertael who told me of Youla's death, a suicide which no one could explain. They had been closer friends than ever I was with either, but I knew the older man well enough, at least, to call him Roger. As the surname suggests, he was Flemish, and during the war, I gathered, had had something serious to do with resistance to the Nazi occupation. Maybe that's how he became acquainted with Youla. He had been trained as a painter but by 1945 had set aside the brush in favor of the pen and was making a modest name for himself as a critic of contemporary art. Youla respected him highly, while Gindertael was unreserved in commendation of his young friend's work. They preferred to see each other en tête-à-tête, I thought, and I therefore met Roger less often than I'd have liked. The few articles by him that Youla showed me were abstruse, phenomenological, difficult to understand. I would have liked to see some of his paintings, but even Youla had not had that opportunity. Never did it occur to me that this rather gaunt, austere, reticent man might make my portrait. And he wouldn't have had he not been in need, living, I was told, at the harsh edge of poverty. His clothes were wretched. Youla asked me if I couldn't do something.

Plenty of French civilians during those years were happily fitted out with impunity in GI attire. For me to do something was easy. With my Military Intelligence credentials I could get almost anything I wanted at the PX. So Gindertael was presently arrayed in olive drab shirts and trousers and an officer's short coat. He was thrilled, did a little dance, and we all drank a lot of wine brought upstairs from the restaurant.

But he wanted me to have some enduring token of gratitude. Possessing nothing material to give, he proposed to offer what remained of his pictorial talent by making my portrait, for he had seen those done by Picasso, Mondain, and Youla and imagined that another, however obsolete in style, might be welcome. I inevitably said yes, though it seemed to bear the taint of an exchange. Unlike the future barter of granny's carpet for Balthus's drawings, however, his was a genuine demonstration of human generosity. I was living then in a comfortable room in a hotel requisitioned by the army. Roger came there one afternoon with his paper and sticks of charcoal. He selected the pose after considering several points of view and carefully arranged the collar of my shirt. The finished drawing shows that he worked not only with confident ease but also with studied attention to the creation of a coherent composition as well as a vigorous image, of which the face, not to mention its expression, is only one aspect of the head, itself the summit of a traditional portrayal.

Gindertael was obviously very familiar with the conventions and attainments of portraiture. His knowledge is evident in the assurance with which he constructed the visual edifice and the skill with which he modeled all of its features into a unified construct of sense data. As a work of art created in 1945 this drawing would have to be

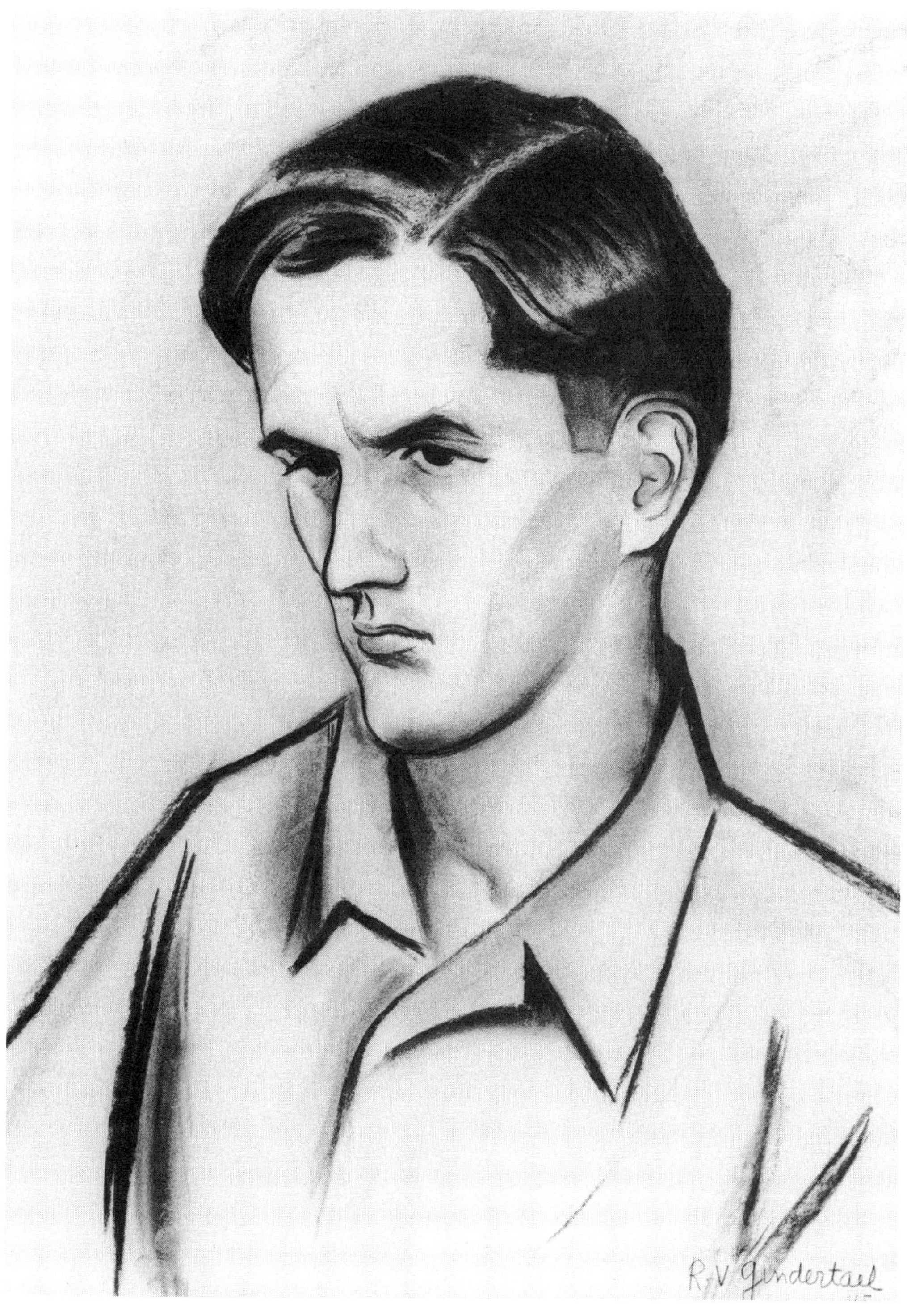
R.V. Gindertael

deemed traditional, but it turns tradition on its head, so to speak, by using the model's likeness, which is sincerely reliable, to make a visual-metaphysical statement solely on the artist's terms. The model is the artist's technical material, nothing more, providing the basis of an autonomous expressive purpose, and Gindertael's use of James Lord is profoundly impersonal. Maybe that is because we knew each other but superficially. Art history was second nature to him, however, so in terms of illusion he knew what he was doing. The portrait is somber, grave, brooding. The eyes are fixed upon something unthinkably grim, the gaze turned inward upon a vision from which in person I discern no aspect of my own awareness. The mouth is set in a saturnine, downturned manner, suggestive of moral stress not ordinarily characteristic of the model. The confident, incisive impress of Gindertael's charcoal, severe, angular, and acute, establishes his sole authority over the significance of the image.

No other artistic rendition of the model's appearance resembles this one. To say that I can't live with it would be narcissistic self-denial, so to speak. To confront it daily, however, would be beyond my power to seize in an act of vision the ideal or intelligible content of a work of art.

I thanked Gindertael sincerely for his drawing and could say with honest appreciation that it was very powerful. I saw him once or twice after Youla's death. Articles by him appeared occasionally in obscure reviews, then ceased. If it is true that I preferred not to confront his drawing very often, nonetheless it has always been framed and I look at it now and then with diffident and self-conscious puzzlement.

MONDAIN

Two days after Picasso drew my first portrait in the Parisian restaurant, I arrived in the remote Breton town of Quimper, a place as far from the fighting as one could get without leaving the Continent. Brittany then might almost have been viewed as but gradually emerging from the Dark Ages, when Celtic refugees reached the peninsula from Saxon-overrun England, bringing a language which fanatic idealists still today endeavor to save from extinction. Along with three other so-called "agents" of the intelligence service, two of them incompetent, I lived in a brand-new villa recently vacated by an owner who had deemed it prudent to leave town with the retreating Germans. We were the only Americans in the area and had little to do save listen occasionally to the ravings of bloodthirsty "resistance" fighters, their legitimacy no more assured than our own. So, in fact, we had nothing whatever to do except drive our jeeps through the impoverished countryside and drink Calvados to excess. Though their putative liberators, the local populace visibly lacked appreciation of our presence. That that was their time-honored attitude toward all strangers, and that Quimper itself was laughingly looked down upon by the rest of France as the quintessential pit of boorish provincialism, we couldn't have known. If we entered a café, the place fell instantly into a sullen hush. It rained nearly without interruption. The shop windows were empty. We soon grew bored and irritable.

Then one wet afternoon I noticed that, of all things, Quimper possessed—in addition to a museum filled with paintings of drowning fishermen—an honest to goodness art gallery, called Saluden. I went in. There were lots of pictures by Paul Serusier, Lucien Simon, and other third-raters of the Pont-Aven school invented by Gauguin, though not so much as a scrap by him. The caretaker of this establishment was an exceptionally pretty brunette of about my age who for a wonder welcomed my chat about contemporary art. She seemed to have a genuine feeling for it, and this certainly came as an exhilarating change from the inane blather of the two twerps in charge of our contingent, even from the Brahmin good cheer of my sole comrade, who later vanished within the black hole of the CIA. Her name was Jacqueline. She told me that there was only a single artist in all Quimper worthy of attention and offered to introduce me to him, not a typical hidebound Quimperois, mind you, but a liberated spirit, born and educated in Paris, living here openly now with a mistress in haughty disdain of convention, a doctor by profession, psychiatrist in fact, chief doctor of the local asylum for deranged men, though devoted primarily to painting and playing the cello rather than caring for the mad, mostly hopeless alcoholics in any case.

A psychiatrist, painter, player of the cello in an insane asylum in a neglected corner at the far limit of Europe seemed too true to be likely, yet irresistibly enticing, akin almost to Kafka. So I said okay,

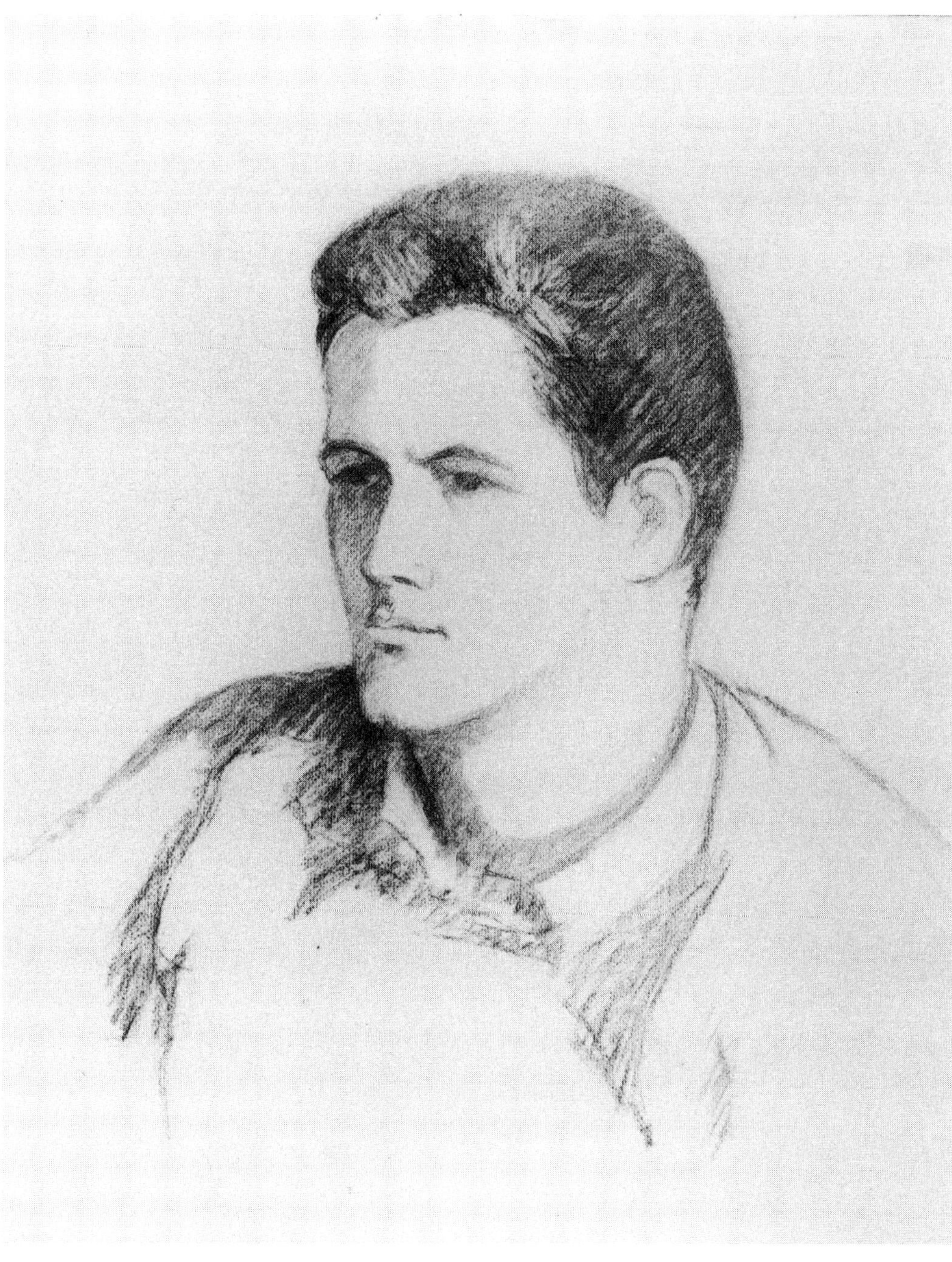

and a few days later we walked up in the rain past the gray, grim, genuine Gothic cathedral over the railway culvert to the high iron gates of the asylum. Jacqueline knew the guard. Dr. Mondain's lodgings were adjacent. He opened the door, kissed Jacqueline on both cheeks, and shook my hand with cordial superiority. A lengthy corridor led to a small salon. The place was comfortable, modest, smelling of rank tobacco. A novel by Céline lay on an oval table. Easel and cello were in respective corners, paintings—clearly by the doctor—on all the walls. These were in a sort of semi-postimpressionist style, a nicely competent alloy of influences starting with Sisley and leading carefully along toward late Monet, stopping short of the cloying water lilies. And that, I thought, was about all. The doctor served an appropriately bittersweet aperitif labeled Byrrh, and informed me that everyone he cared to frequent—the happy few—called him Pluto because he considered his appearance similar to the dog of that name in the animated cartoons of Walt Disney. To be sure, he was of countenance plain but not quite canine, though the name, I later learned, suited him very well for mythological reasons. That, however, has little to do specifically with portraiture. Inevitably we talked about art. Pluto's unassailable criteria began with van Eyck and favored Jean Clouet as the most likable of all portraitists. When I mentioned Picasso, he sneered. When I said that I happened to have with me at the commandeered villa a portrait of myself drawn by the famous painter, the doctor compassionately smiled, allowing that someday he might feel disposed to make something appreciably more serious.

After a few further singularly enjoyable visits to the asylum, after meeting Mamouche, Pluto's mistress (everyone in his realm received a nickname, mine in time becoming Jamouille), and having a couple of her exceptionally excellent dinners, when food was difficult to come by, one afternoon in an unprecedented plunge of sunshine the doctor sat me down on a stiff chair to draw my portrait. Having been shown the Picasso, he had declared that a Montmartre sidewalk artist could have done better.

He drew with charcoal on a good-sized sheet of paper, studying my features repeatedly as he slowly worked. It took quite a long time, an hour perhaps, and it was clear that the image did not come to him with spontaneous ease. Nor had it ever done so, he remarked as he worked, for the likes of Holbein or Dürer. When he had finished, however, I was surprised, because the portrait looked better than I had expected, or for that matter had had any reason to expect. What surprised me most was an ever so faint reminiscence of slightly similar drawings executed by Picasso a couple of decades before. Pluto's work was of another universe of achievement, certainly, and yet the reminiscence was there. I thought the portrait flattering, convinced I had not so fine a face. Snapshots of the period, however, suggest that this is, after all, an acceptably close likeness. How lucky I was not to believe myself good-looking. The portrait pleased me all the same, and I said so. To tell the truth, at first I liked it more than Picasso's sketch. It wasn't as good, but I liked it despite the deficiencies in dexterous finesse so noticeable now. The doctor made me a gift of his drawing, though he didn't sign it, and I have kept it safe for fifty-seven years, though never consecrated my appreciation with a frame.

Today, I occasionally lift the drawing from its portfolio and wistfully gaze at it like the illustration of some story about the fanciful,

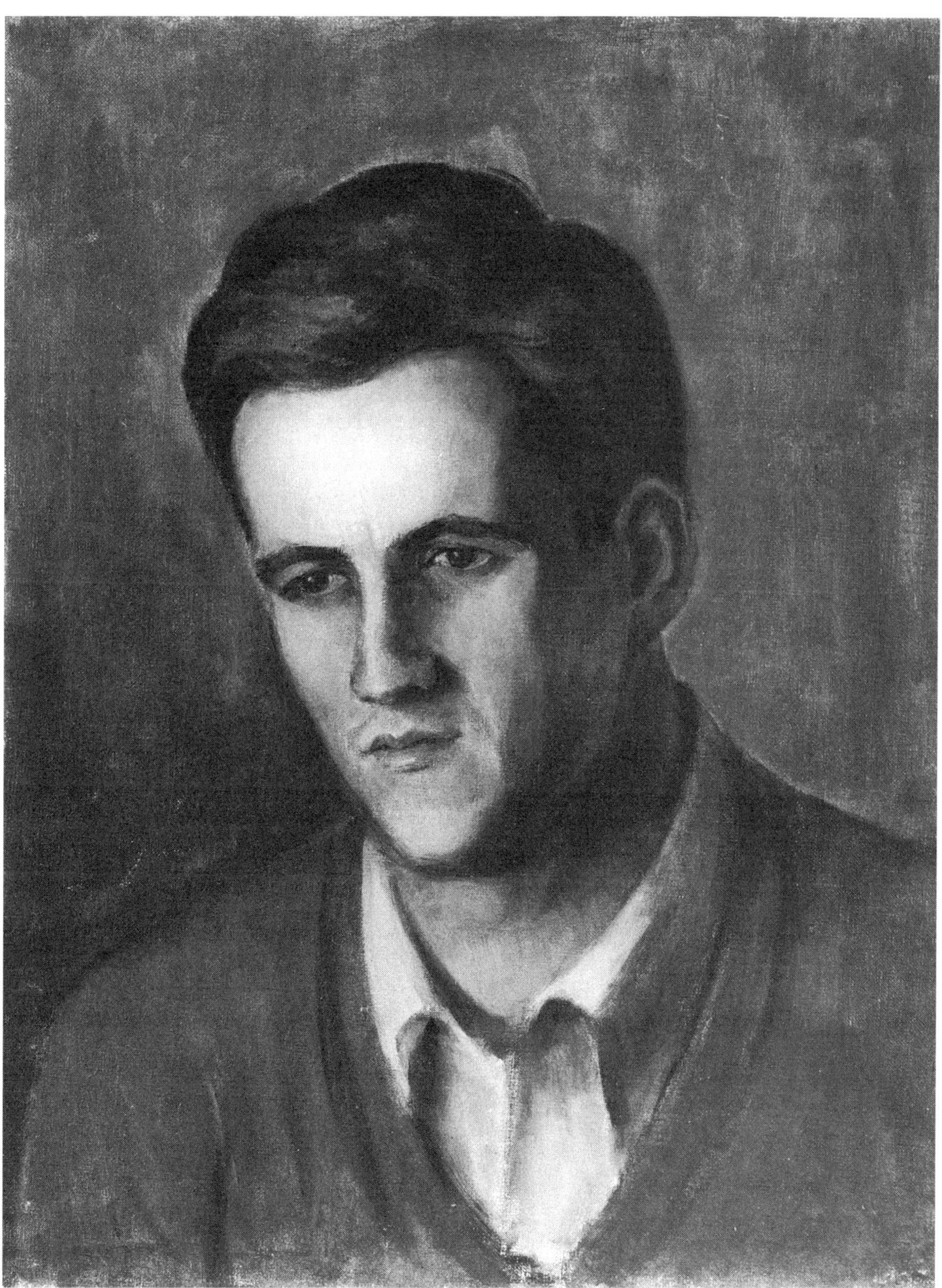

long-forgotten adventures of some anonymous youth. There is no metaphysical statement here. The portrait's paradox, indeed, resides in the mystery of relations between artist and model, model and artist, and the semblance—a semblance only—of idealization with an image which in reality owed very little to the overt conduct of either. The mystery turned out to be superficial, trivial, perverse. The principle of illusion is given no grace in this drawing, which is nonetheless a work of art, because there was on both sides, at least, a surmise of surrender to the transubstantiation of the creative act. But there is no self within the image to interrogate my own searching gaze. From the frontier of the quest I come back to myself unfulfilled. There is no revelation in terms of experienced time, because no authentic commitment of human nature was made on either side. At the moment I was foolish enough to feel otherwise, but I was very, very foolish then, in any case, and understood absolutely nothing as yet about the satisfaction or fatality of portraiture. Nor, needless to say, did Pluto.

Our relationship when the war was over proved to be relatively prolonged, ultimately preposterous, and quite akin, indeed, to Kafka. Off and on I lived for more than a year behind the asylum gates with the doctor, his mistress, her son, and her mother, though only Pluto cordially—but a little too cordially, as it turned out—enjoyed my presence. A long story, in short. Irrelevant today. He made many portraits of me, some more effective than others, though none of true distinction. Still, they all bore some residue, however wanting, of that redemptive longing for imperishable identification with the incomprehensible progress of human life. Reproductions of two will do.

The second, a painting, was executed sometime in the early autumn of 1947. It loses nothing by being reproduced without color. Less assured in finish than the drawing of two years before, it is perhaps in concept more ambitious, but the artist's effort to endow his vision of my visage with psychic—precisely!—penetration remains limited to the pictorial surface, as his laborious representational skill was insufficient to render the expressive structure of that most enigmatic constituent of the human anatomy: the head. Even at this very remote remove, however, and despite the faulty draftsmanship, I can recognize the aim of the gaze of a youth well advised to be pensive. What I think to discern behind, or within, those disturbed eyes is a glimpse of unrewarded searching for an avenue into unlimited experience. In a word, freedom. Pluto, I believe, was little concerned by this essential aspect of his model's persona. Had he been, he would hardly have ventured to portray a person with whom intimacy took itself for granted. The doctor deemed his discernment more truly knowing than my own, but he was mistaken and his painting shows why. It is the work of a person playing at creativity in order to fabricate an image of himself which eludes him, which conceals, indeed, the pursuit of that evasive but veracious vision which is the real raison d'être of portraiture. The paradox here, though patent, is not a pretty one. Of all the model's features, only the mouth appears to have received the artist's attentive concentration, but even the studied sensuality of the lips is, by contrast, confounded by the incorrigible aggressiveness of the chin.

If this portrait shows, as it does, less assurance than the earlier drawing, that is because less conviction lay in the artist's hand. Youth, the imaginative perseverance of youth, had ever so fitfully been frittered away for the sake of an ideal impersonation. Cavalier defiance of convention's common courtesies, albeit the rule of psychological omniscience, comes at a cost computed by malevolence. The doctor was dismissed from the sinecure in Quimper and assigned to a position of lesser laissez-faire and harder work at an asylum for women in the drab, porcelain-producing town of Limoges. He callously cast off the previous mistress and her family, not to mention a few friends, applied himself without prosperity to the reincarnation of the sometime Pluto, and anon was abandoned in turn by a newfound mistress, who went to the bother before departing to slash every last one of the canvases saved by her lover in utopian memory of a more complacent potentiality. He retired when required to, contracted cancer, died, and is remembered today with some wonderment and little esteem by very few.

BROWN

The model portrayed in the drawings by Roger Gindertael and Theophilus Brown is the same person and even the poses are somewhat alike, though in the latter portrait the head is raised higher and in every respect the facial expression is dissimilar from that in the work executed four years previously. If one did not know that in both portraits the model is the same, it would be understandable to see in them the likenesses of two different young men whose resemblance to each other is apparent but superficial. That Gindertael worked in the harsh medium of charcoal while Brown used the gentle tone of pencil does not affect the extreme diversity of the two portraits. If any evidence were needed—and it is not—that artists portray themselves as well as their models, and perhaps with more unsparing exactitude, then it is here in the comparison of these drawings. To try to say which is the finer work of art, leaving aside consideration of personal appreciation, would be irrelevant. I have mused upon the similarities and dissimilarities between the two only because they are chronologically adjacent among the portraits made of me and because the contiguity seems provocative, not to make sensuous judgments relative to either one.

That Bill Brown and I became acquainted was more or less inevitable, we being of about the same age, Americans in Paris in the late forties (when there were few), companionable with many of the same French friends, and preoccupied by similar professional aspirations. Theophilus was the forename of Bill's father, and he later adopted it in public for naturally distinctive reasons. He was living, as most of us were, in an inexpensive room in a modest hotel not far from our café haunts. It was there that he drew my portrait one afternoon in early November of 1949. It is a tentative token of things to come, for Brown has devoted himself principally to portraiture with subtle distinction and an appreciative measure of public appreciation for half a century. The drawing of me is executed with gentle sensitivity and studied competence. The likeness is touching rather than striking. There is no hint of flattery, but neither is there any suggestion of indifference. The twenty-seven-year-old model is not handsome; his features appear simply pleasing because they radiate a sense of search and purpose. From behind those pensive eyes I can glimpse myself peering in the direction of the future. The gaze is the likeness, a revelation which Alberto Giacometti was exploring at the very same time.

Artist and model obviously saw eye to eye, as it were, concerning the objective of a portrait, and on the evidence of very different ventures apparently still do, fifty years after the fact. Their searching identification with this apparition was essential to the extent that the veracity inherent in art needs self-surrender fused with self-command for the sake of a living likeness. It is a proud and presumptuous undertaking. When true to itself, however, it cannot then be false to the heartless opinion of time. I see my portrait by Theophilus Brown as enduring proof that a cooperative metaphysical resolve can create a feeling and natural statement about human experience.

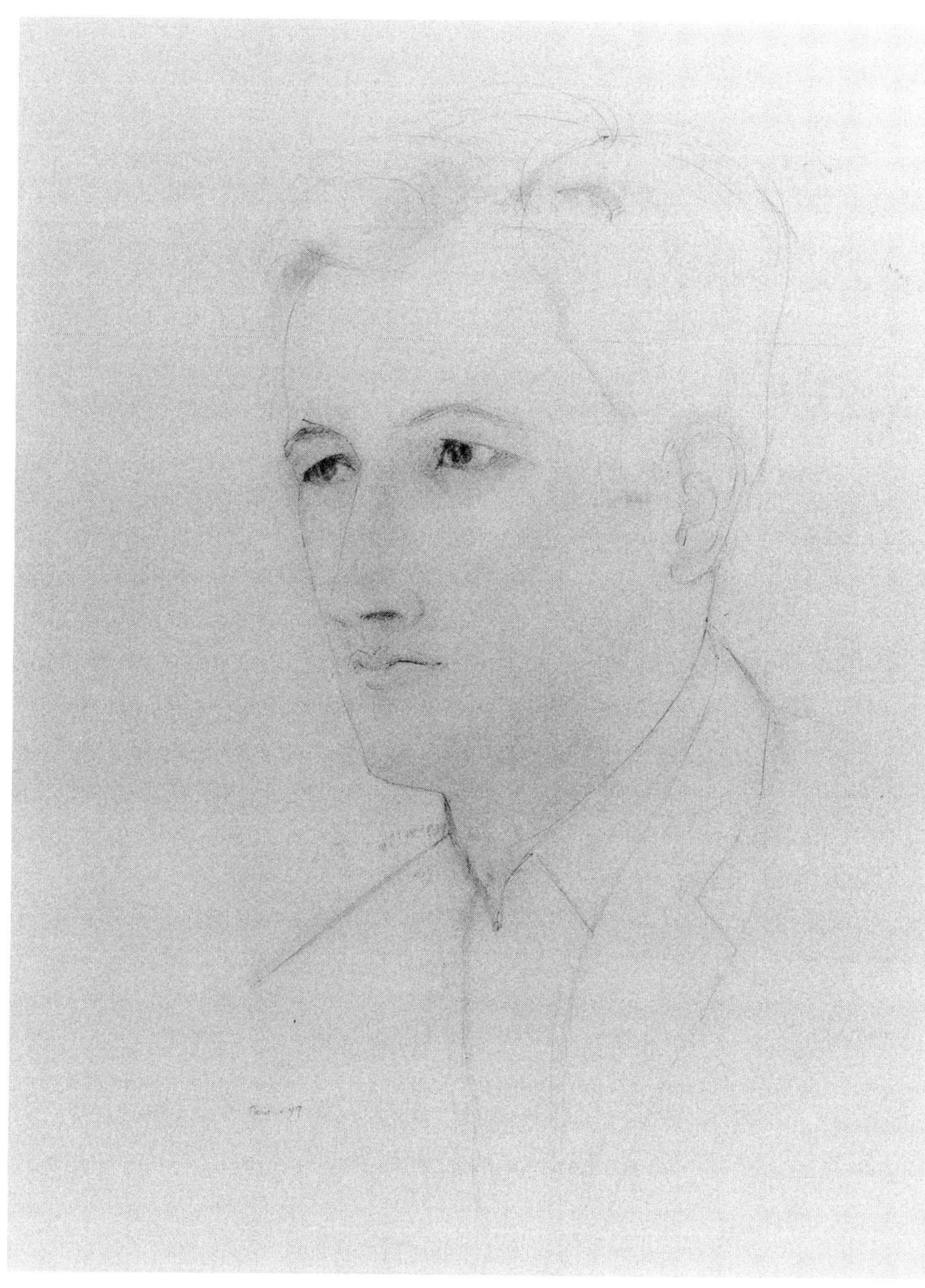

FREUD

On the eleventh of October, 1949, I traveled from Paris to London, where I remained for two weeks. That fortnight had a durable effect on my life to come, because I met an exceptional number of people whose friendship altered my view of myself and widened the prospect of potential fulfillment for me. Two of them were artists, John Craxton and Lucian Freud, both of whom made drawings which will be illustrated here. Exactly the same age, Lucian and John had for some time shared a studio and at that moment were the happiest of colleagues. I felt fortunate to be invited to participate in some of their uninhibited camaraderie. Lucian enjoyed a modicum of specialized celebrity, being the grandson of a world-famous and authentic genius, the founder of psychoanalysis. This lineal good fortune seemed at the time to be of atavistic benefit to the young painter's professional reputation. Already at age twenty-seven he was considered a creative personality of unusual promise, and his rare paintings and drawings—for he then worked with excruciating slowness—were admired and acquired by a few discerning connoisseurs. He had arrived in England from Berlin as a child of ten, but never outlived the memories, heritage, and influence of Mitteleuropa at a time of direst crisis. John, on the other hand, was the happy-go-lucky offspring of an immemorial British family, the son of a distinguished musician and teacher, and so he grew up in a milieu of cultural security encouraging to creative purpose. Thus, though molded by decisively different surroundings, Lucian and John were for a time perfectly compatible young artists. I had the opportunity to admire works by both of them in the apartments of individuals like Peter Watson and Cyril Connolly. Personally, I preferred jolly and easygoing John, but Lucian did possess a compelling aura of exotic excitement and potent self-assurance. I was glad to think of them as newfound friends, since I had few, and wrote them letters when I returned to Paris. Not much later I achieved a note of prestige by having a story published in a distinguished literary review called *Horizon*, and it earned compliments from my London friends.

Lucian was the first to turn up in Paris, having been to Vienna with a friend to place a plaque in honor of his grandfather on the house at 19 Berggasse. He had been seriously impressed by my story, he said, and invited me to pose for a drawing. It was pointedly made clear that the invitation came as a mark of high consideration. Even then Lucian was not diffident about the distinction his artistry could confer. Why he chose to honor me with his talent I never knew, and a guess today would be supererogatory. But I was in luck, because he was working then at the unsullied summit of his superlative creative skills. The sessions of posing took place in a very small room high up in a hotel without elevator on the Île de la Cité. It contained a narrow bed, one chair, a wardrobe, and a sink, nothing more. I sat on the chair, Lucian on the bed about three feet away with his draw-

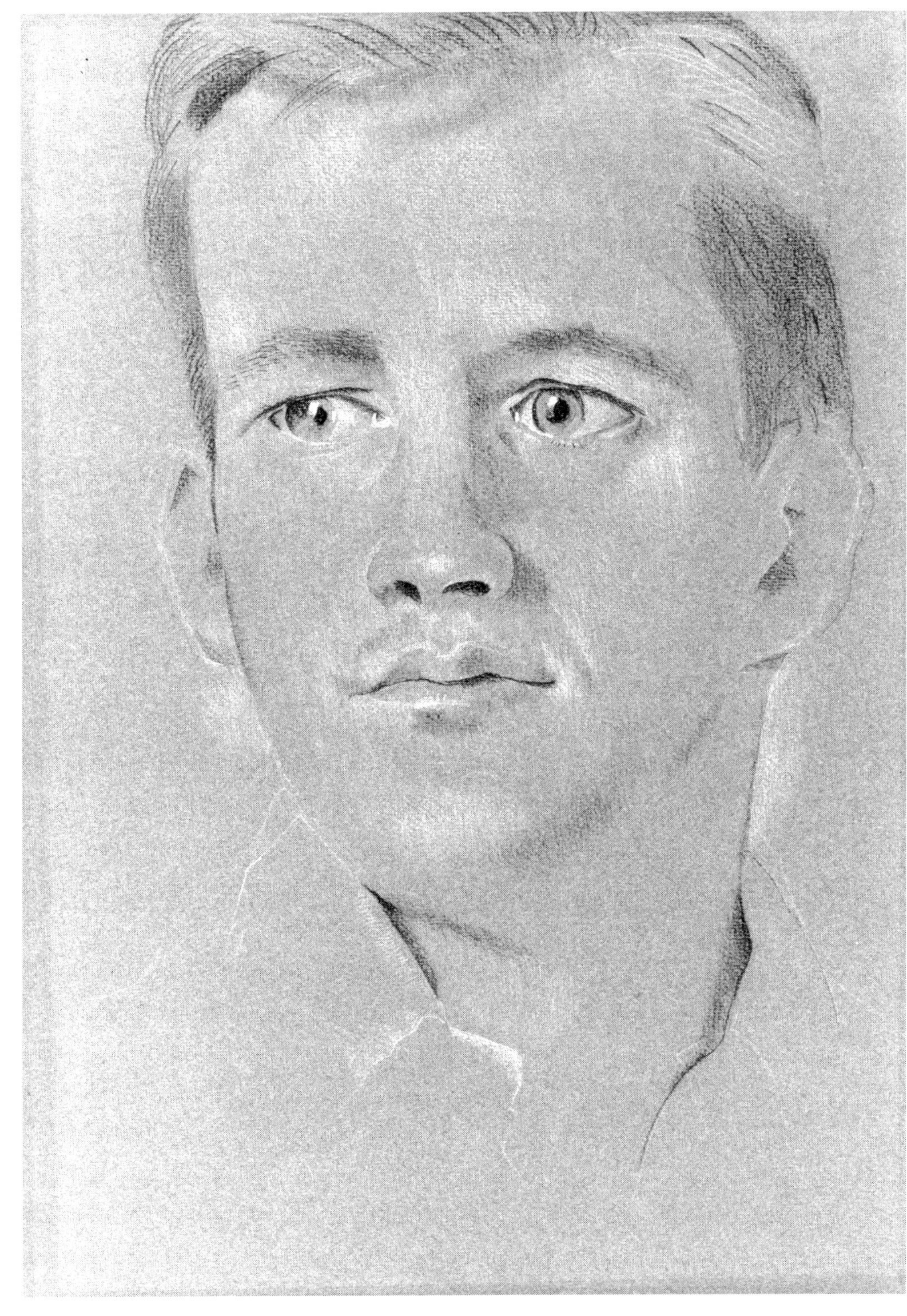

ing pad on his knees, working on a sheet of dark brown paper with pencils of black and white chalk, which he sharpened frequently with a razor blade. Posing for Lucian was the most peculiar and exacting experience I have ever known of that very specialized commitment of one's physical and mental state. Not that I felt displeased, not at all; I was only aware from the first of something strangely different about the entire procedure, even about its outcome, and time and chance have done nothing to alter this sentiment. In the first place, Lucian did not simply study my features with searching intensity while I, of course, at his insistence remained absolutely immobile. He positively stared at me, as if to achieve by some extrasensory retinal perception a physical grasp of my face. If this was, to say the least, disconcerting, what was far more so was his repeatedly rising toward me, though he was only a few feet away, until his eyes were but two or three inches from some part of my face, and then persistently studying it as if he were peering into a microscope. After which he would resume his former position and usually make but a single dot on his page. This bizarre concentration, accompanied by no comment, was seriously unnerving, but I, too, kept silent. I had a sense, however, that we were engaged, artist and model, model and artist, in some sort of arcane contest which I had never before associated with portraiture, and never did.

Then there were the surprisingly frequent visits to the toilet, which was located somewhere outside the room, though I never knew just where because I never had need of it. Each session of posing lasted for two hours or so, during which Lucian would two or three times suddenly rise and announce a trip to the toilet, but before leaving he would carefully place his drawing under the bed so that I could not see it. I was taken aback by the odd conjunction of urinary urgency and care to conceal his work, which he might easily have taken with him if he had sincerely desired to prevent his model from glimpsing the work in progress. After all, I might easily have taken the drawing from under the bed for a quick peek if I'd wished to. Lucian was always absent for four or five minutes. I never thought to betray his bizarre compulsion for concealment. It seemed to be a stratagem in a contest between artist and model, and I had a feeling that if I touched the drawing Lucian would somehow know I'd done so. As for the urinary urgency, I thought of it then only as an inconvenience, but in subsequent years I've known people to visit the toilet frequently for reasons of physical comfort, so to speak, having nothing to do with the bladder. I have no idea that this may have been Lucian's motive, but the visual evidence of his work at the time makes the possibility tantalizing. At all events, I believe that the artist and his model were then untroubled friends. One afternoon Lucian asked me to accompany him to a workshop where prints were being pulled from an etching he had made a couple of years before. Called *Ill in Paris*, it is considered by some critics his finest work in the medium. A few proofs were made, and Lucian gave me one, inscribing it, "For James, with love from Lucian." I was pleased and grateful, and still am.

A few days later Lucian announced that he was obliged to return to London. I had been posing for about a week. He considered the drawing uncompleted but wanted me to have it as a souvenir of friendship, though he would not sign an unfinished work. I was delighted by it and very pleased to have it as it was. I had seen in London a portrait drawing of Peter Watson by Lucian that was very highly finished and had felt that the obsessive precision of every detail took life away from the model for the sake of the image, in which each strand of hair could almost be counted. My portrait I believe to be one of the finest drawings of Lucian's early period, which in my judgment is indisputably his best. And it is fine, I think, not because it is a faithful image but precisely because it is not. However, it is a striking resemblance executed with such remarkable finesse that no reproduction can convey its visual intensity. The resemblance, though, while verifiable, is more *about* the model than *to* the model. The image is not that of a mask lifted as if by some esoteric alchemy from the visage and set upon the page. The hallucinatory fixity of the eyes reveals how ardently and helplessly the real-life model behind that mask sees his unreal situation: i.e., that the mask may be seen as a life mask, not as a lifelike aesthetic creation. At the time I was unaware that for some years previously Lucian had been obsessed with portraying dead birds and animals. Death, in any case, was inevitably much in the forefront of Jewish awareness only five years after the unforgettable, unthinkable revelations of Belsen, Treblinka, Auschwitz, and so many ghastly similar places.

Lucian never hesitated to make self-willed metaphysical statements. During the first ten years of his artistic maturity he stubbornly and laboriously—one might almost say desperately—expended his creative powers upon portraits which are possessed by a masklike semblance with hallucinatory, outsized eyes. "A moment of happiness," he said, "never occurs in the creation of a work of art." Indeed, he made his purpose even more explicit by declaring, "The task of the artist is to make the human being uncomfortable." A painstaking scrutiny of his lifework compels the observer to surmise that in this ambition he has been successful.

It is not fitting here to try to analyze the value or evolution of Lucian's career. One must acknowledge, however, that in the course of it, especially at the beginning, he produced some superb portraits. Later he adopted a much looser, almost expressionist, style which has found ample favor with critics, who have praised him as one of the greatest portrayers of the individual human being in the whole history of art. The author of the catalogue of Lucian's exhibition at the Whitechapel Gallery, Catherine Lampert, placed Freud's portraits on the same level of quality as those of Rembrandt. No exertion could compete with the weight of that opinion. And yet one wonders how any artist living today could bear such a burden with equanimity.

COCTEAU

Jean Cocteau tried his hand at everything, and in everything he tried his hand at he proved prodigiously talented. When aged but twenty-three, Diaghilev had said to him, "Astonish me!" He took the admonition so seriously that one might say it swept him off his feet to such an extent that he never regained his gifted equilibrium. He certainly trod the high wire between talent and attainment, with no face-saving net below, and still today his silhouette trembles in midair, a graceful but ambiguous figure extolled by some, dismissed by others. His lifelong idols were Stravinsky and Picasso, men of certified genius whose achievements he yearned in vain to emulate. They were entertained but annoyed by his mercurial praise and expert pirouettes, yet when he died they both acknowledged an irreparable loss of spellbinding virtuosity. His life was like that. It has been recounted and analyzed by several biographers. Even I have related aspects of it, so there is no need now to revisit this well-traveled terrain.

One summer afternoon in 1950 on a Mediterranean beach Picasso urged me to make the acquaintance of Cocteau, offering his recommendation as an infallible calling card. The meeting came about by accident, and Picasso was right concerning the efficacy of introduction. Cocteau was cordial. He invited me to visit him at the villa of a wealthy lady who used her famous guest and his beautiful boyfriend as verification of her status as a freethinking patroness of the arts. I accepted, and it wasn't long before I looked like an accredited friend of the attractive trio, Jean, Doudou, and Francine. A more courteous person than Cocteau would even then have been difficult to find, today next to impossible. His manners were like a minuet by Mozart. In his propensity to please there was almost no length he was unprepared to traverse. And maybe he went too far.

Nearly everyone who knew anything about Jean—and in France there were few who knew nothing—knew that in addition to his countless other talents he was an accomplished draftsman. Already in 1923 he had published a volume of his drawings—dedicated, of course, to Picasso—most of them portraits of friends, Poulenc, Radiguet, Nijinsky, Diaghilev, and, inevitably, Picasso himself. They are purely linear, skillful, original, striking likenesses, at times akin almost to caricature, immediately recognizable as the work of a remarkably intuitive hand. These were Jean's finest works as a draftsman. Other volumes followed, plus dozens, hundreds, and eventually thousands of incidental drawings as the skillful hand matured in facility like a phenomenal plant rising from the floor of a rain forest in unconquerable momentum toward the vital nutrient of the sun. By the time every fashion magazine featured the occasional drawing by Jean and his works could be purchased for something close to a pittance, there was no mistaking his distinctive style or the easy originality of his images.

During that first summer of our friendship, Jean offered me sev-

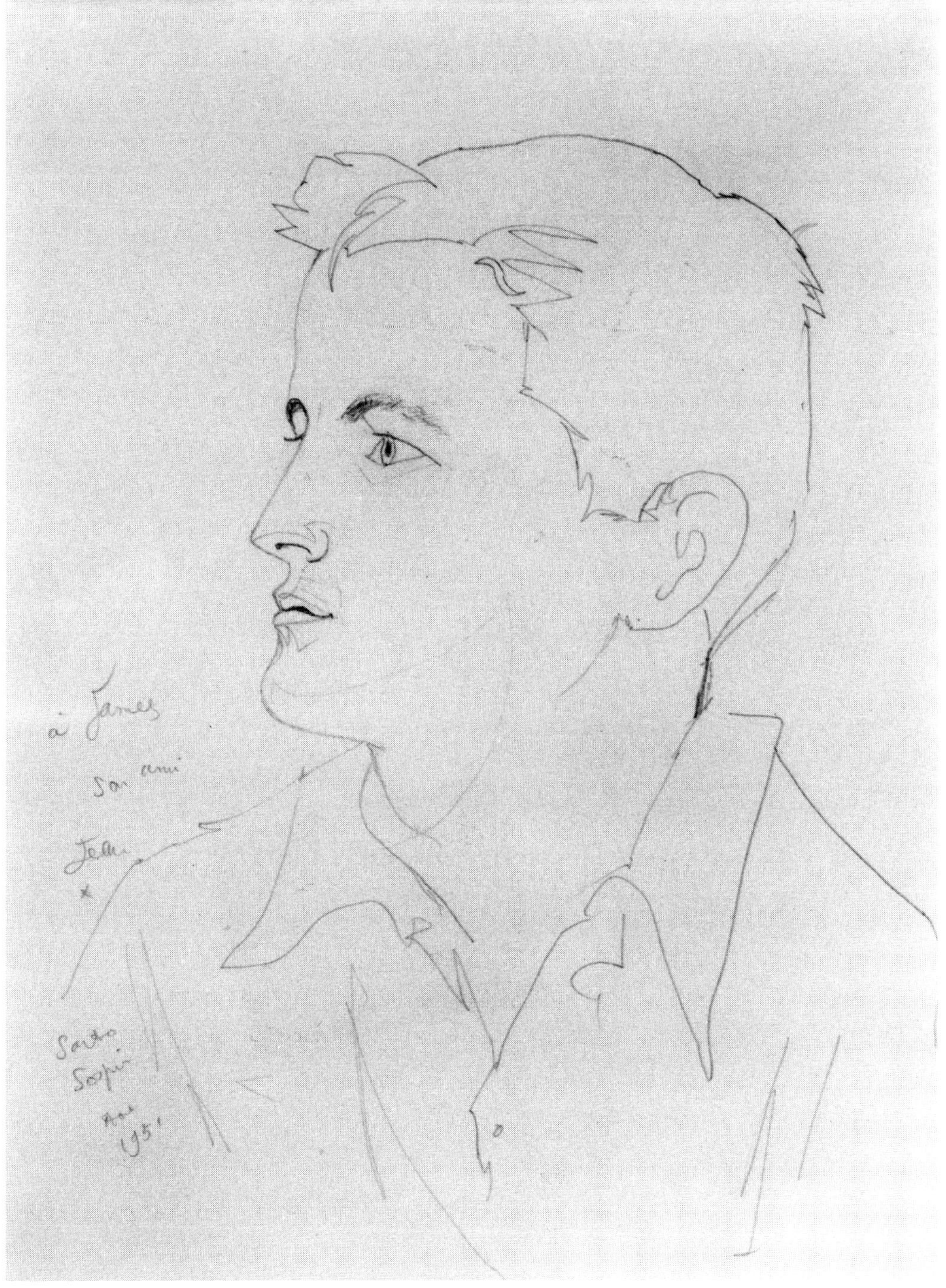
à James
son ami
Jean
Santo Sospir
Août 1951

eral drawings. They procured honest pleasure at the time and do so still today. I have known no other artist who so prodigally and politely offered his talents and their productions to almost anyone who showed a modicum of appreciation, and even to quite a few who didn't.

The following summer I found Jean and Co. installed as before in the opulent villa of Francine Weisweiller. We went for afternoon cruises on her yacht, dined at the Hôtel de Paris in Monte Carlo, even visited Picasso in Vallauris (much to his snide displeasure). And one afternoon in August, Jean sat me down on his bed and announced that it was high time he drew my portrait. The pose chosen was a profile. The work took but fifteen or twenty minutes. Jean by that time had executed so many portraits that a basic formula always lay ready at his fingertips. Still, he concentrated on his model and his drawing. Not an artist to be taken lightly, he possessed a style that insisted on itself and had long since learned to catch a likeness. The portrait he drew has a luminous, instant appeal, and the fashionable tricks of draftsmanship confer a facile, static resemblance. But the artist was more alert to the enjoyment of drawing than to its outcome. Certainly there isn't the slightest semblance here of metaphysical intuition, though Jean in his journal at the time was much concerned with flying saucers and supernatural phenomena. The human object of experience in space and time as distinguished from a thing-in-itself remains fixed immutably upon the page, revealing in detached contemplation no inference whatsoever as to the glorious truth which art can wring from nothingness.

As a portrait the drawing possesses a certain charm which in every respect reflects the artist's own inimitable charm. Charm, moreover, is not a characteristic to be dismissed out of hand. That is why Jean's portrait of me can still ignite a flash of sensuous pleasure after fifty years. But his power to charm was not what Jean had labored a lifetime to demonstrate. He aspired to master his sensational facility. Too intelligent, however, to hide from himself the self so captivating to celebrants of foolproof fame, he must have seen in the end that his self-portraits, of which there had been many of many varieties, were dazzling but deficient images of spiritual endeavor. Ever nimble on the tightrope of disillusion, he would perform yet another brilliant pirouette, never allowing a misstep of frustration to disfigure the distinction and audacity of his performance, which is why he was so likable.

MAAR

About Dora Maar, her life and my relations with her, I have already written a book of more than three hundred pages, and therefore will endeavor here insofar as possible to limit my comments to a consideration of her solely as an artist. That, after all, is what she was from first to last, and few people more than I owe it to her to emphasize that fact.

A young, ambitious, emancipated woman eager to make a name for herself in the visual arts, Dora conscientiously attended art school but hesitated between painting and photography. The camera had only recently conquered for itself the prestige of creative invention which pencil and paintbrush had held inviolate for six hundred years and more, and since then, of course, photography has been borne higher and higher upon the crest of fashionable popularity until today the click of a shutter can produce an image prized by earnest connoisseurs as a work of art equal in aesthetic effect and monetary price to a Corot or Picasso. This is why I have chosen here to present one photograph and one drawing of the same model by the same artist.

Dora opted for photography. She possessed an instinctive eye for what was picturesque, perverse, or even pictorial, and rapidly learned how to exploit her camera, manipulate negatives to produce surprising effects, and capture images of human pathos, abstruse empathy, or satire. The surrealists soon noticed that her work could be seen to exemplify some of their symbolic, dreamworld hocus-pocus, and she was willingly drawn into their realm of unbridled and manipulative license. Before the age of thirty she was well known in esoteric circles. Of all her creations, the photographs of this period are those most sought after today. It is not as a breeder of the bizarre, however, nor as an emotional inquisitor of anonymous subject matter but specifically as a portraitist that Dora is evoked here. Even in the time of her recherché originality her rare photographic portraits were conventionally fashionable: facile, tricky likenesses of the rich or famous. Then she became Picasso's mistress, and her former profession was set aside save for the celebrated series of photographs of her lover at work on the enormous canvas of *Guernica.* Pencil and paint replaced the camera, presenting a more redoubtable challenge to the eye than the quick and flexible medium of film. One of the difficulties in characterizing as an artist a producer of photographic portraits is the absence from the finished image of any evidence of the maker's creative option. The camera is indifferent, unsurprised, unresponsive. The eye behind the lens cannot convey a subjective, ontological view of the model as an objective, mutable human being. In the photograph the model is static, isolated from the world, past, present, and future, sealed outside of time like a prehistoric wasp in a blob of amber. A photograph, consequently, cannot tell the truth about the model, because the portraitist cannot infuse the image with his, or her, own truth. To be

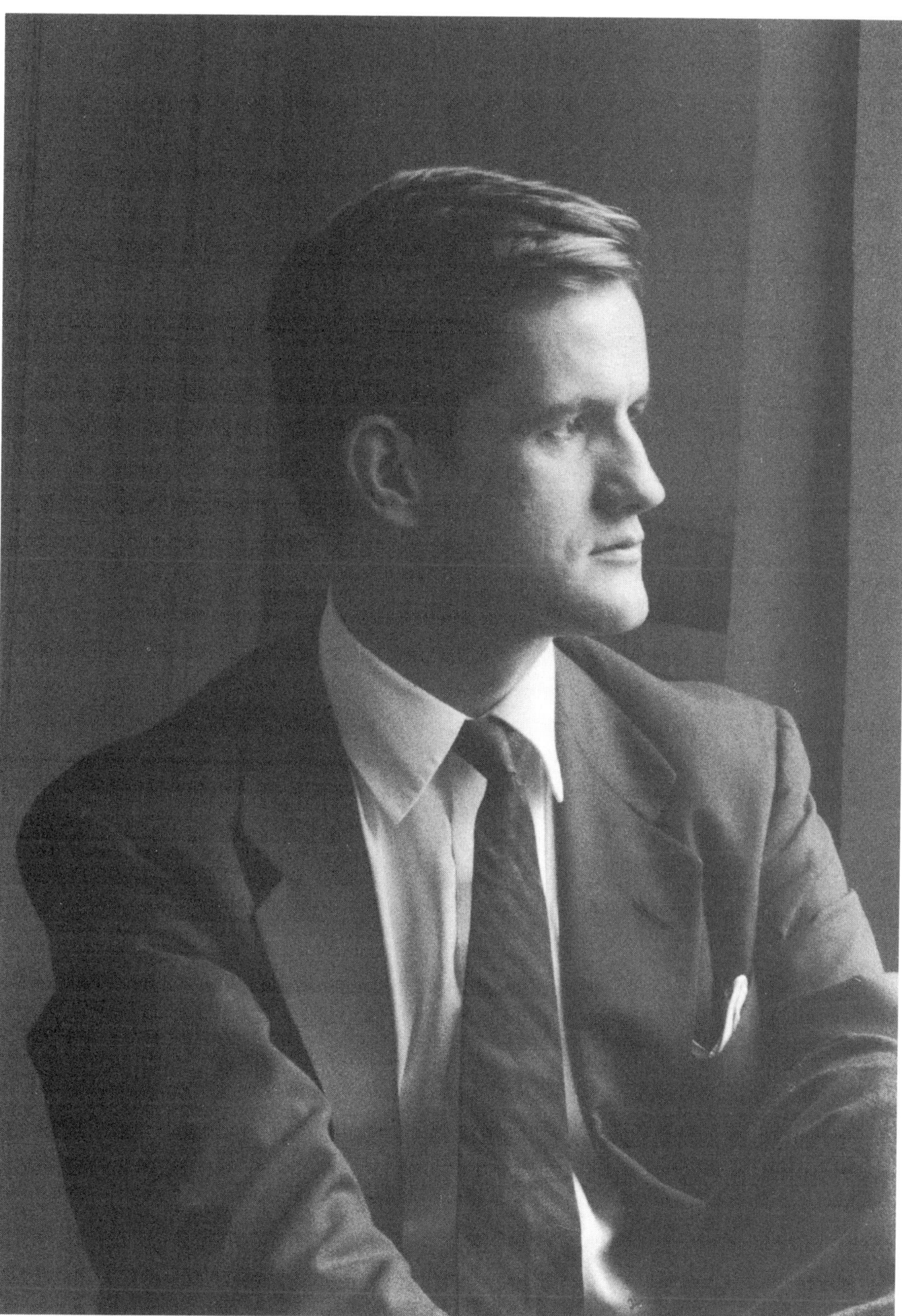

sure, a photograph is better than nothing, because it offers to surmise the semblance of individuality, but it can never subsume the vitality and veracity, however compromised, of a work of art. It makes no metaphysical statement and offers no suspension of doubt in regard to the principle of illusion.

It was some years after the period of our closest intimacy that Dora offered to produce a photographic portrait of me. I needed one for the jacket of a book, and she generously proposed to make it. The drawing which follows was executed earlier, but photography was Dora's beginning profession, and an example of her work in that medium seems appropriate to contrast earlier and later objectives in representation. Oddly enough, I will subsequently have the opportunity to consider a similar juxtaposition with, so to speak, reverse results.

Dora's photograph is a snippet of likeness clipped from the velocity of time. It will never change or offer an intimation of metamorphosis. The model's motionless expression says nothing about his temperament or raison d'être, while the photographer has made no commitment whatever of personal feeling. That is the protective trick of the camera, because this photo, after all, could lose itself among a million images of anonymous people without anything individually essential on either side of the lens being lost. We see merely an approximate picture of a young man who appears to have been sensitive, well-bred, and pensive but might just as well have been a cunning maniac meditating murder.

Between 1953 and 1958, Dora made six or eight drawings and paintings for which I posed, and I have chosen to reproduce the one I had entirely forgotten but which seems to me today to have most to reveal about artist and model, their relations, and the meaning of portraiture for both. It was executed during the summer of 1954 at Ménerbes in the house given Dora by Picasso, and of all the portraits she made of me it is the only one I did not receive as a gift. So when I finally came to write a memoir of our friendship I naturally had no inkling that for forty years she might have preserved any likeness of me for her private and lonely scrutiny. After her death in 1997, aged eighty-nine, the forgotten drawing was perfunctorily marked with an auctioneer's stamp and sold in the hateful dispersal of all Dora's belongings—including even her hats, gloves, shoes, and shoe trees! The purchaser, a friend of long standing, chanced to recognize the model and generously made me a gift of my portrait. Thus, I now possess at last this drawing which for reasons known only to her secretive self Dora had wanted to keep hidden always from all eyes save her own. As soon as I saw it, though, I felt I could guess why she had wished not only to preserve it but also, and above all, to prevent anyone else, and me, perhaps, in particular, from perceiving what sensitive strength of feeling the portrait had wrung from the artist. At the very moment of creation, I suspect, Dora must have been astonished to see what she had done, for the model's likeness is rendered with such a revelation of the artist's own emotional tenderness that it is a disclosure which reaches frankly beyond affection. How unlike the fossil of the photograph. How unlike any other portrait of me ever made. Less skillful and brilliant than some, to be sure, but by the very token of a deliberate determination more moving. All doubt in regard to the principle of illusion is here absolutely dispelled. Dora at the same time was becoming more and more deeply committed to mysticism, and her drawing is a profound

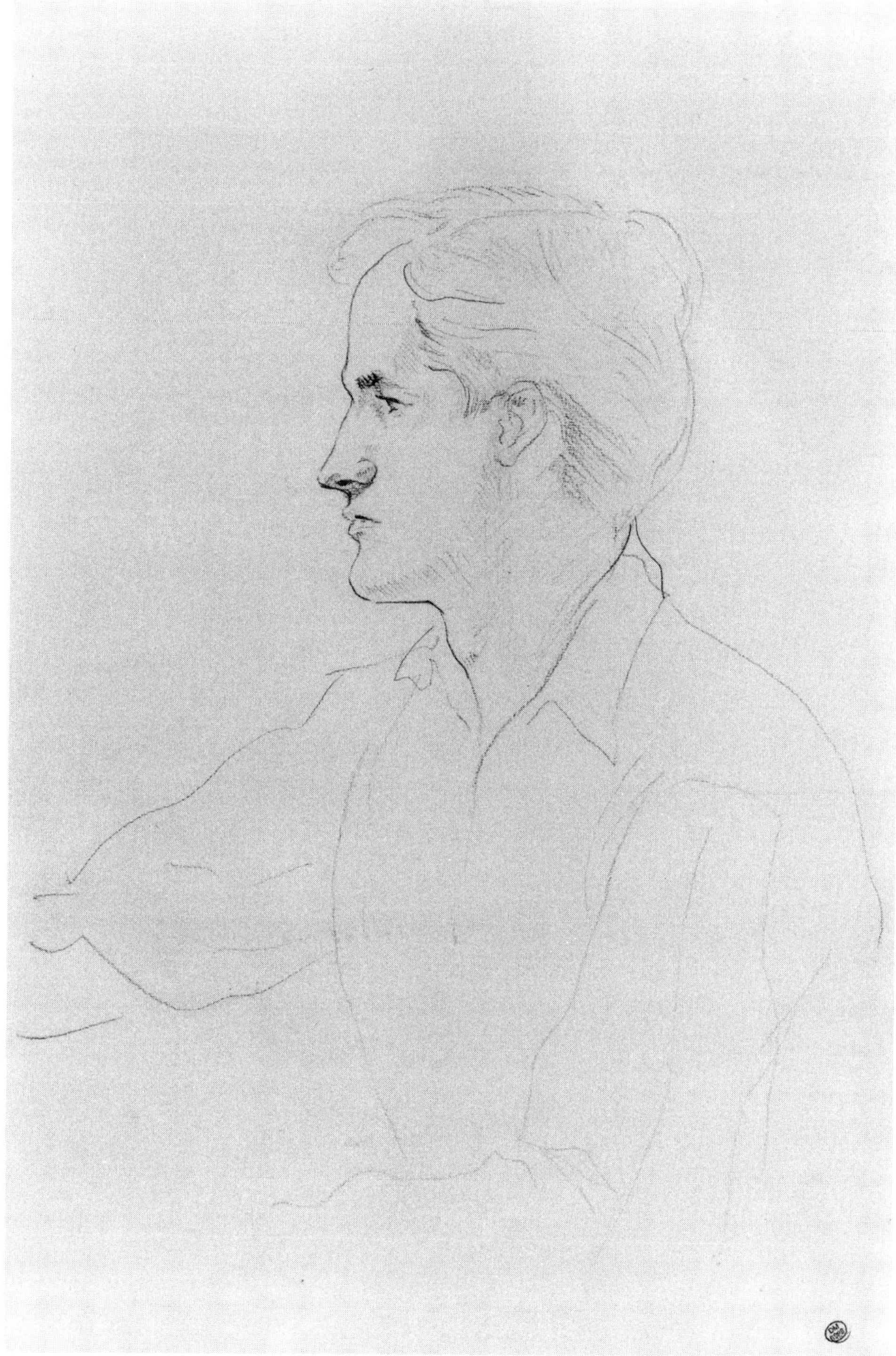

metaphysical affirmation. It is meant, and what it means is especially meant, to endure forever. The quivering delicacy of the features, the expression of thoughtful noblesse, the grace and poise of the model's surrender to the artist's contemplation: all these multiplied by each other contribute to an image of timeless truth, the vindication and consummation of the life of art.

When I look at this portrait today, remembering all the mornings, evenings, afternoons that Dora and I spent alone together in that grand old wreck of a house in Ménerbes, and recall how I wondered at the time what might be done to make our friendship perfectly right, I believe the knowledge lay patiently in wait for me all the while, like a beast in a jungle waiting to spring while unknowingly and unsuitably I was fated to pass it by. If at the time the artist and model had both devoted dispassionate diligence to contemplation of that portrait, then perhaps their friendship might have had a different dénouement. Who knows? Dora is dead. But her portrait of me survives as poignant evidence of art's power to penetrate the mysteries of the human heart.

CRAXTON

In the summer and autumn of 1946, John Craxton and Lucian Freud traveled together from England to Greece, and were there intoxicated by the Homeric sea and honey-colored air after the grim anxieties of embattled Britain and the drab austerity of postwar hardships. For John the exhilarating felicity proved lifelong, and to this day he remains, ecstatic, on the island of Crete. Lucian, on the other hand, even at age twenty-two, craving greater glory than had been current in Greece for two thousand years, hurried home in search of it.

Except for the occasional homeward visit to the selfsame house in Hampstead where he was born, John has stayed on in Greece. His painting, at which he has worked with happy creative license whenever so inclined, has not earned him celebrity but, rather, the thoughtful respect of his peers and of conscientious critics. His early work shows reminiscences of Picasso, though no intent to take visual advantage of the master's protean and provocative inventions. John's work has always been gentler, more joyful and humane. The Grecian honesty, easy passion, and mythic imagination have been Craxton's stylistic symbols from the beginning. If in the early work there is visibly more vigor and lyrical ingenuity, that is the momentum of youth. Its velocity naturally grew quieter and more thoughtful in time. Far from the maddening throng of mountebank scribblers and money-mad manufacturers of fame, John has contentedly produced paintings of shepherds, goats, fig trees, fishermen, sailors, soldiers, and the fragile residue of a culture which in half a century has sold the soul of Socrates to the American Express company. His paintings are precious relics appreciated by the happy few who can visualize the timeless meaning—the metaphysical revelation—of an aged peasant on a donkey making his way up the face of a cliff in search of firewood.

John was always lavishly generous with his work, because he considered its value in terms of friendly and feeling appreciation, never as a source of cash except when his Spartan circumstances called for a little. From the beginning he offered me paintings and drawings, which have illuminated my homes for fifty years. I traveled occasionally to Greece, he passed now and then through Paris. It was not until we'd known each other for five excitable years, and shared a few volatile adventures, that he proposed to draw my portrait.

Once again I posed in the narrow bedroom of a modest hotel. John rapidly produced a pleasing, though somewhat conventional likeness. It satisfied me at once, but he didn't agree, insisting that my features wanted a more intense stylistic interpretation. I pleaded for the portrait to remain as it was, as I was later fated to do with Alberto Giacometti, to no avail whatsoever in either case. John erased what he had done and set about composing the highly stylized image which we see here. The recollection of cubism hovers over it,

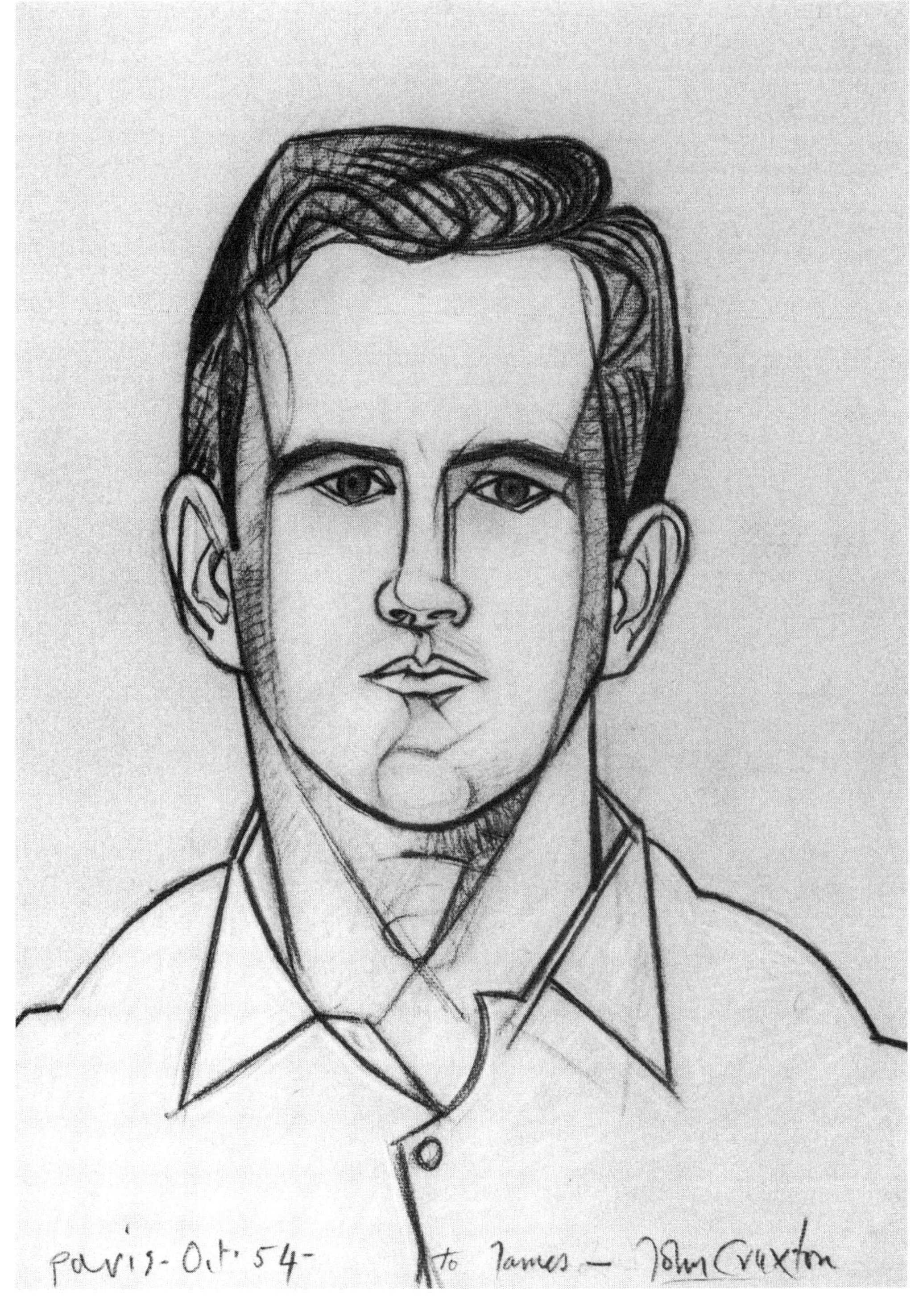
paris - Oct. 54 -
to James — John Craxton

and yet the draftsmanship is vigorously individual. Were it not supposed to be a portrait of myself, I could admire it as a work of studied and dynamic originality. But it fails as a likeness, and its aesthetic truth is technical skill, not imbued by the sunlight of Apollonian harmony. Still, I am fond of the drawing because it was made with pure conviction by John. Happily I own another portrait made by him, this one a likeness of himself painted in gouache some years earlier. It is a beautifully realized image of the artist in the full faith and freedom of his creative vision, a testimony to the redeeming ideal of human fulfillment glimpsed long ago in Greece.

GIACOMETTI

It seems literally quixotic that I should sit down today to write yet again about Alberto Giacometti, having already written more about him, I think I can say without boastful exaggeration, than anyone else. But the last word, the definitive statement, the conclusive judgment is never pronounced so long as it concerns a great man, and even less should he have happened to be a creative genius. Despite the evident premonition of impertinent redundancy, then, and prepared, indeed, to gamble with crude repetition for the sake of verisimilitude, I'm willing to risk invective by writing about Alberto as a portraitist, having already done so more than once. But, after all, of the twenty-four artists whose portraits of myself I have the temerity to discuss here, Alberto made many more than anyone else and expended upon them the truest testimony of his genius, leaving in them the greatest metaphysical affirmation of the phenomenon of portraiture. As a matter of fact, I'm happy to have the chance to write once more about Alberto.

Of the several thousand drawings executed by him during his brief lifetime (sixty-three years and three months) many were no more than hasty sketches, meant for the discipline and memorization of his eyes alone, but hundreds of others, highly finished, were deliberately autonomous works of art, intended to validate an aesthetic concept, and of these a great many were portraits. Portraiture, indeed, became the ultimate purpose of his entire creative endeavor. His models were almost exclusively persons whose lives coincided intimately with his own: his mother, first and always; his brother Diego likewise; his mistresses; his wife; and an approximate score of friends whose more or less frequent presence in his studio the artist strictly put to artistic use. If drawings are, as they are, the most intimate, spontaneous, and revealing expressions of an artist's sensibility and intelligence, then they will also provide the surest measure of his achievement. Drawings tell the truth about an artist. Perhaps this is so because drawing is a universal activity. Children tracing faces in the dust or adults limning in air the outlines of a body are seeking the draftsman's truth. Insofar as surviving works provide basis for judgment, it is apparent that the greatest artists have invariably been great as draftsmen, and indeed, that no artist has been truly great who was not a great draftsman. Since an artist's drawings reveal him as he is, it is the character of his care for truth which determines the quality of his drawings, and the power of perceiving truth is inseparable from the power of expressing it. In this context one must acknowledge that artistic truth is the fundamental truth of humankind. From the beginnings of civilization it has been the human likeness which has most preoccupied man. What we seek and value in a work of art is its relevance to human life, its emotional and intelligible relation to a representational vision of a living being. In short, a portrait is an artist's most profound and expressive response to life. Alberto's resolve was to endeavor by

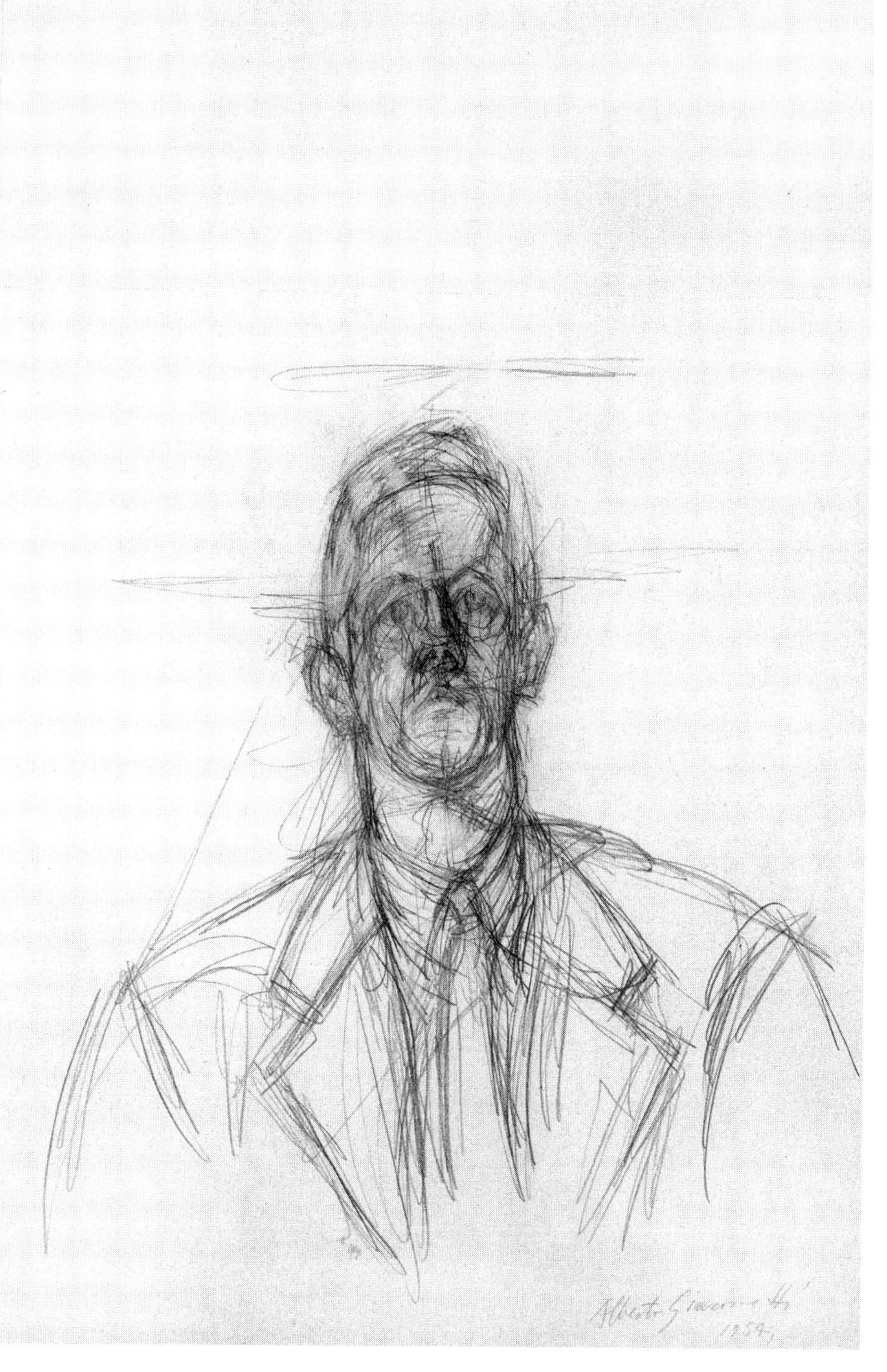

means of art to make known what is unknown and, having done that, to try to preserve such knowledge from death and oblivion. His portraits do this by looking beyond a mere likeness into the space where infinite surmise offers but a tantalizing inference as to the durable, verifiable reality of a human presence.

It was only a week or so after being drawn by John Craxton that Alberto asked me to sit down and pose for him. Why he did this I'll never know. Maybe it was because I'd lately been seeing him fairly frequently, as I was then engaged in writing a long essay about him and his work for the first issue of a new magazine devoted to the arts called *L'Oeil*. This was my initial struggle to put into words what I imagined I understood about Alberto's creative undertaking, and I needed to appeal to him for insight. He was patient and generous, as always, although my understanding was faulty and insensitive. But there I was, often underfoot, and he asked me to pose. I was thrilled by a sense of unique privilege, which even then I realized would have made Alberto laugh.

The first drawing he made is the first reproduced here, and it is the most powerful of all those he drew of me. By power I mean to suggest the dramatic aesthetic intensity with which he imbued the image qua image as a work of art comprising an immediate visual experience separate, if possible, from a simultaneous, deliberate, and conscientious determination to create a portrait. If one looks quickly at this drawing for the first time, one sees immediately and only a Giacometti, a forceful work in his mature style depicting a man's head and shoulders. The individual behind the expressive, graphic impression appears almost as a wraith wrought from the strong, probing skein of the artist's pencil. And yet Alberto always sought to disentangle a likeness, though sometimes the wisp of resemblance was perceptible only to those who had also seen the model. And so in this first drawing I do ultimately peer outward at myself from the overpowering medium of Alberto's style. It is as if he saw in my appearance from the beginning an incipient vigor and vitality contained within an aspect of violence of which I was unaware. While he was working, Alberto peered at me constantly. The action of the artist's pencil and the concentration of his gaze could be construed virtually as a unified creative process. It was obvious that his drawing depended absolutely upon my willing submission to its priority, and on the evidence of what he did Alberto clearly saw more in his ingenuous model than I could have perceived in myself. *What* he saw is in the drawing, which, after all, is not only a Giacometti but also a portrait of stunning stylistic originality. Truth to the totality of visual sensation was the basis of Alberto's creative commitment as a draftsman, painter, and sculptor and that is what sets him metaphysically apart from the other artists of his time. Thus, the evocative, tantalizing first portrait of myself produced by Alberto's passionate concentration is a prototype of the veracity inherent in art itself. He signed and dated it at once and gave it to me. I was almost paralyzed by gratitude, though managing to stammer some thanks, which the artist hurriedly shrugged away. He could do better, he said, and asked me to come back the following afternoon to pose again. I took the drawing home, tacked it to the wall of my bedroom, and considered myself transfigured into a state of being hitherto unknown.

During the ensuing days, a week or more, I went every afternoon to the rue Hippolyte-Maindron and sat before Alberto on a

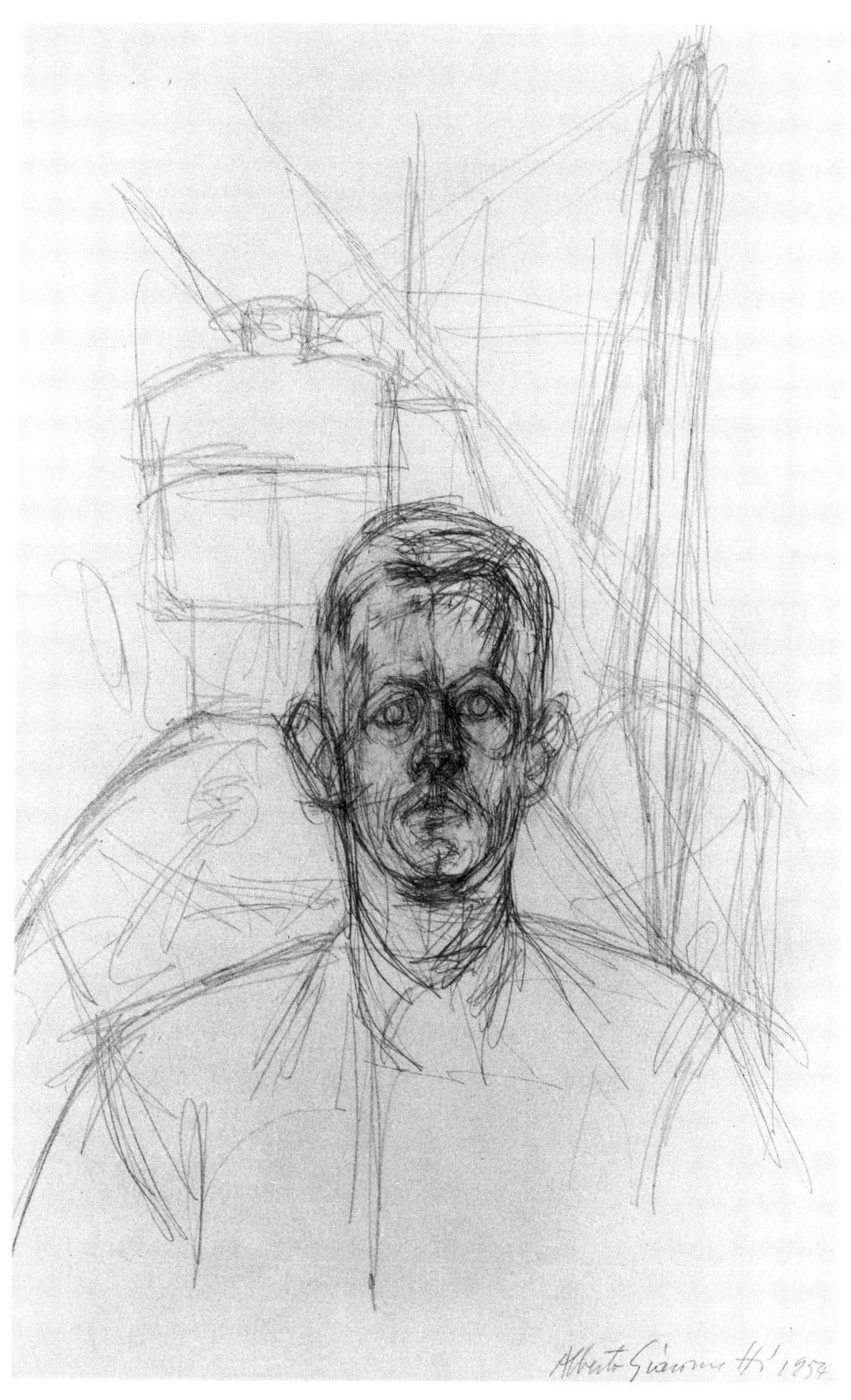
Alberto Giacometti 1954

wicker café chair while he made drawings. I can't remember now in what order these later portraits were executed or how many he produced—twelve or fifteen, I'd guess. But I did make copious notes in my journal of our conversations, because Alberto was a tireless talker as he worked. What he said, however, was so similar to his talk while painting my portrait ten years later, all of which has been published already in *A Giacometti Portrait*, that there would be no point in duplication here. Still, I can never forget with what astonishment I first heard Alberto's sincere lamentations concerning the hopelessness of ever achieving what he sought to do and the lacerating but exhilarating sense of failure with which he lived from day to day.

Of all the portraits drawn of me by Alberto, then or later, the one most often considered finest by connoisseurs and curators, and even, I suppose, by myself, is the drawing reproduced next, executed in the autumn of '54 in the same series as the first. To be sure, it offers an impression of careful finish due to Alberto's habit of frequently depicting objects and surroundings behind the model, creating an image which seems complete because it is placed in relation to a situated space. Though this may not be immediately apparent, the objects surrounding my head and shoulders are, to the left, the early sculpture called *The Spoon Woman* and, to the right, a tall, slender female figure typical of those Alberto was producing at the time. It has been suggested that my position between these two sculptures was deliberately chosen by the artist in order to emphasize a rapport between two very unlike representations of nude women. This is nonsense. My position was determined entirely by chance, and it would have been utterly out of character for Alberto to stage a mise-en-scène in order to "illustrate" diverse aspects of his work. This second drawing happens to be an excellent and typical example of the visual change Alberto brought henceforth to his works of portraiture, particularly in drawings. Till then he had not been much preoccupied by physiognomic exactitude. Now he became increasingly so, even in sculptures and paintings, which present more complex conceptual difficulties. The difference between the first drawing and the present one is striking and significant. Though both are unmistakably recognizable as works by Giacometti, the first harks back to an earlier stylistic mode, while the second, executed not long afterward, conveys a different spirit altogether. The artist has receded, the model has come closer. The art of inferring from outward appearance the inner character and temperament of a model, even in the case of his mother or his brother, had not till now engrossed Giacometti. From 1954 onward, however, it was the essential presence of the human being as it appeared to him that he sought to reveal by approaching ever nearer and nearer to the living presence of the model. And yet he persistently asserted that he had more than enough difficulty in depicting a person's exterior without troubling himself over what lay within. He recognized, in short, that he had finally reached the frontier of impossibility, where life and death conjoin, and this awareness would add measureless vitality to his creative stamina.

If this second portrait is Alberto's finest drawing of me, it has always been the one I liked most and believe to be most likable. Here my presence is immediate on the surface of the page. My nose, in fact, appears to jut physically forward from the sheet of paper, a sculptural effect which Alberto constantly endeavored to create, and luckily felt that he endeavored in vain, for this delusion led to infi-

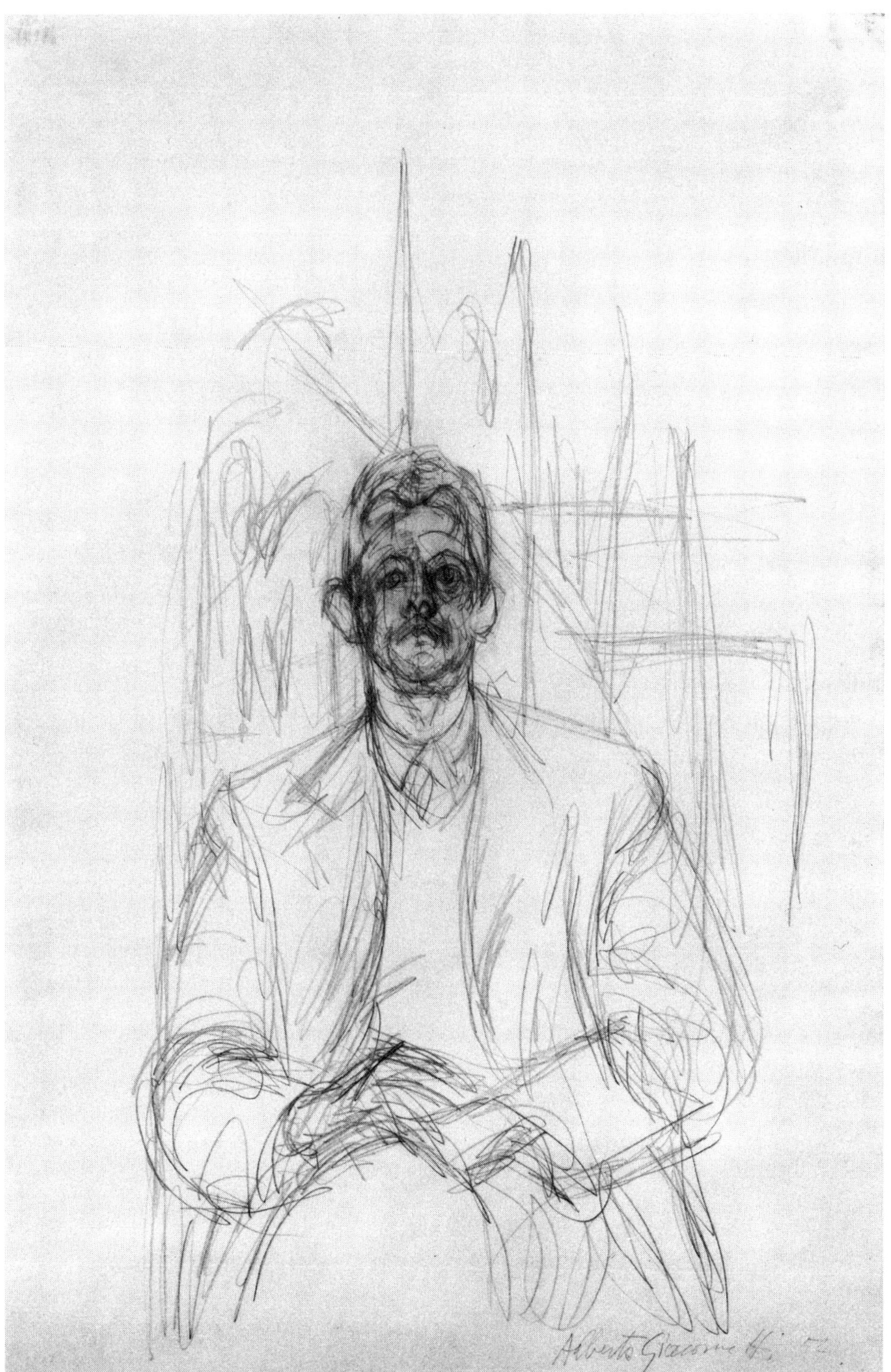

nitely renewed endeavor. Giacometti's models were invariably required to look the artist straight in the eye. To him the human gaze was the purest, most personal, most intense manifestation of the living being. My gaze is unflinching and vivid, directed intently toward the viewer, outward and penetrating, yet imbued with deep inner emotion and surmise, profoundly true to life at its most marvelous and mysterious. To be absolutely truthful to the fleeting reality of visual experience was Alberto's foremost, lifelong resolve as an artist and a human being. Truth, he said, interested him even more than art. The ultimate criterion of artistic truth was the accuracy and sincerity of retinal sensation coupled with the logic and necessity of its plastic expression. In this second portrait of a modest admirer Alberto clearly found fulfillment, for the likeness to lived life transcends both the skilled self-sacrifice of the artist and the emotional submission of the model. It is an amazing and moving revelation of one man's dogged but doomed determination to compel reality to do his bidding. To me it is not a comment upon civilization but simply a vital aspect of it, and myself an incidental, perishable particle of a whole which no one can understand.

The two other drawings reproduced here are stylistically similar, though neither is comparable in profound creative concentration to the second. Still, they are interesting and reward study by demonstrating what variations of perception Alberto's visual perseverance could produce. In the third drawing the model is placed at a further remove from the viewer, and from the artist, than in the second, showing the complete torso, both arms and hands crossed upon a knee. The background, being less specifically defined, seems, if not confusing and ineffectual, at least somewhat arbitrary. And yet the drawing is an excellent one. Purely as a portrait, indeed, it may seem more satisfactory, though less dramatic, than the second precisely because of the spatial separation between the viewer-artist and his model. The head, being smaller, does not challenge contemplation with such an astute and penetrating command, and yet the resemblance is immediately recognizable. The image, however, is not intimidating. I see myself with composure and a certain self-satisfaction. Though the gaze dominates, it does not overpower the likeness or demand metaphysical meditation. The second portrait is intellectually compelling and emotionally forceful, while the third is placidly pensive and feelingly peaceful. Models as unlike as Peter Watson, Jean Genet, and Igor Stravinsky remarked that when posing for Giacometti a sort of romantic aura grew between artist and model. I certainly felt this to be true, and I believe Alberto felt likewise. Though he never said so, his behavior spoke for him, and the third portrait conveys—to me, at least—a sense of reciprocal warmth. And perhaps it is meaningful that for this drawing—and for this one alone amongst an approximate score in all—Alberto chose a sheet which on the verso already bore another drawing. Maybe he had run out of clean paper, but there were numerous sheets in his portfolio that must have held for him a less personal meaning than the one he selected, because it was on the rear of a very powerful, beautifully finished portrait of himself that he chose to draw yet another portrait of me. So we are united in time and space on the same sheet of paper, and if his gaze could pierce the page, which would not be surprising, then he sees through his vision of himself his vision of a dreamer and admirer whose life would be transformed utterly by his friendship. I do not believe that this exis-

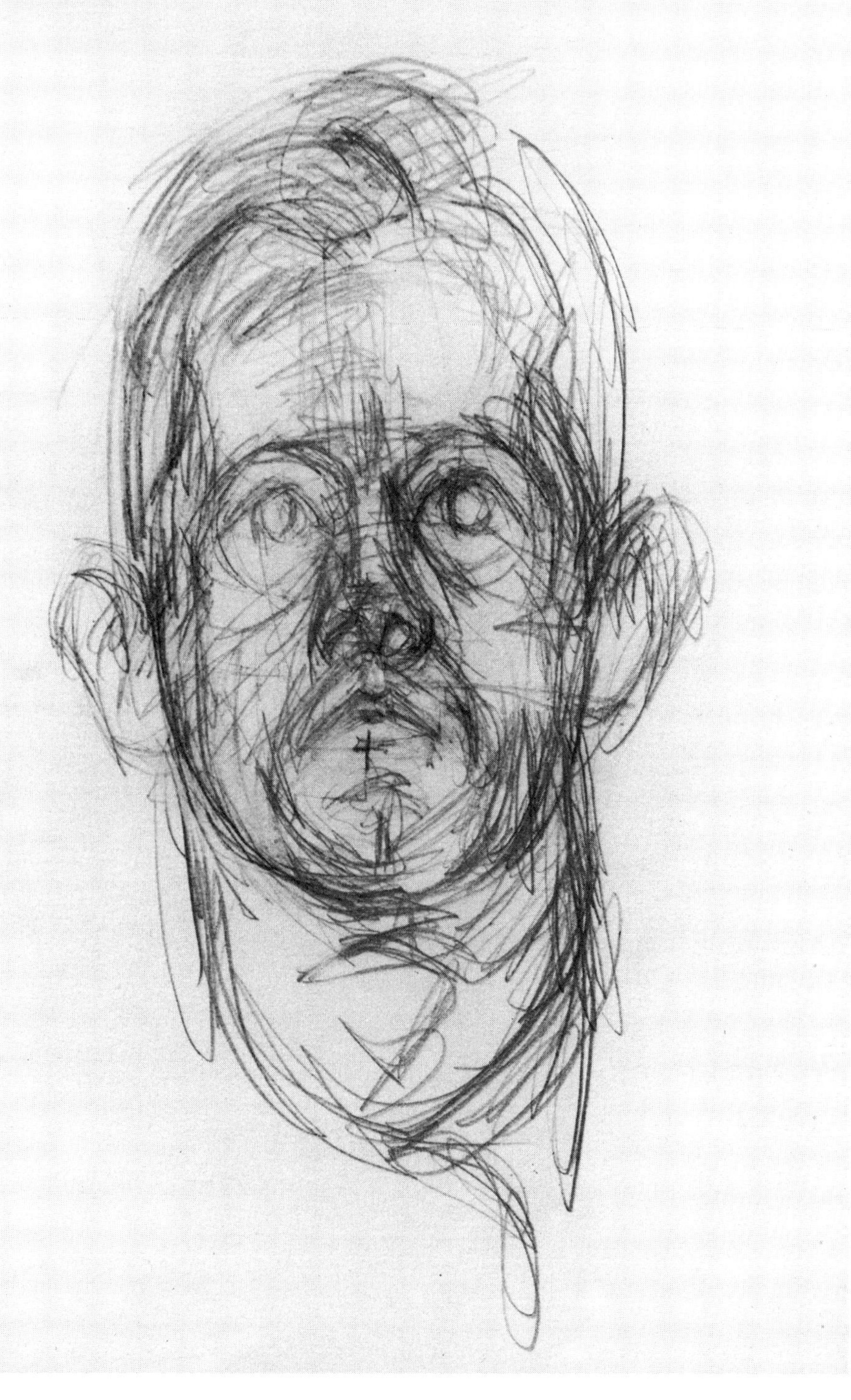

tential juxtaposition can be categorically attributed to accident. If it were, then our lives would be ruled by biology alone. Amongst Alberto's drawings there are quite a few that bear works on both sides of the sheet, but I know of no other self-portrait which he put to use, as it were, in order to mirror his vision of someone else. When it came to signing this work, another gift to the model, he placed his name and the date beneath my portrait. His own features, to be sure, needed no signature.

The fourth and last portrait drawing I have chosen to reproduce is an illustration of Alberto's absolute visual veracity via the form that most preoccupied him all his life: the human head. Here we see my solitary head, isolated in space, set autonomously alone in the center of the empty sheet, which can be construed as a semblance of the cosmos. It defies definition. After several years of semiabstract work in the early 1930s, Alberto had resumed purely representational work, especially the study of the head, and for this reason was drummed out of the silly surrealist sect by André Breton, who said, "Everybody knows what a head is," when in fact a head is what is most puzzling and enigmatic about us all as soon as one peers beyond a commonplace configuration to contemplate its expressive mystery, its look that looks at the act of looking and its power to control the use of vision. For Alberto life was sight; seeing and being were equivalent. In this head study the model's gaze again establishes his vitality. The essential structure of life is centered upon the eyes. This conviction was the metaphysical absolutism of Giacometti's creative courage. It was not for nothing, he said, that the first benevolence offered to the dead is the closing of the eyes.

Alberto made hundreds, probably thousands of studies of heads, many of them from memory, the majority being of his brother, his wife, his mother, a few friends, heads that he knew well but felt he always failed to truly grasp, render, or understand. He nonetheless never ceased trying, and it was in the indomitable splendor of his failure that Alberto proved his greatness, for it is precisely by the power with which an artist offers us a glimpse of the invisible that he can compel us to see our truth, too, in his vision of it.

Ten years after drawing that first series of twelve or fifteen portraits, years during which he occasionally drew still others, Alberto remarked, as if it were a comment on the weather, that I might pose for a painting. Needless to say, I said yes. Work began a few days later, on September 12, 1964, to be precise. From the beginning I kept an exceptionally detailed account of exactly what was done and said during those eighteen momentous afternoons that I spent with Alberto, posing, talking, and visiting the neighborhood cafés. This account was later published exactly as I had written it at the time, save for a few labored efforts to improve awkward phrasing, and there would be no point in repetition here. However, I didn't try to envisage my portrait then specifically as an exemplar of portraiture. And indeed when Alberto sat down to paint in 1964, his concept of what it took to produce a likeness had undergone some change from the view which had determined his dynamic creativity of ten years before. In the thirty-seven years since then my own notion of what portraiture represents in general, and this portrait in particular, has also inevitably undergone revision. So perhaps I'm a little at liberty to risk some tentative surmise about a picture I've been looking at for half a lifetime.

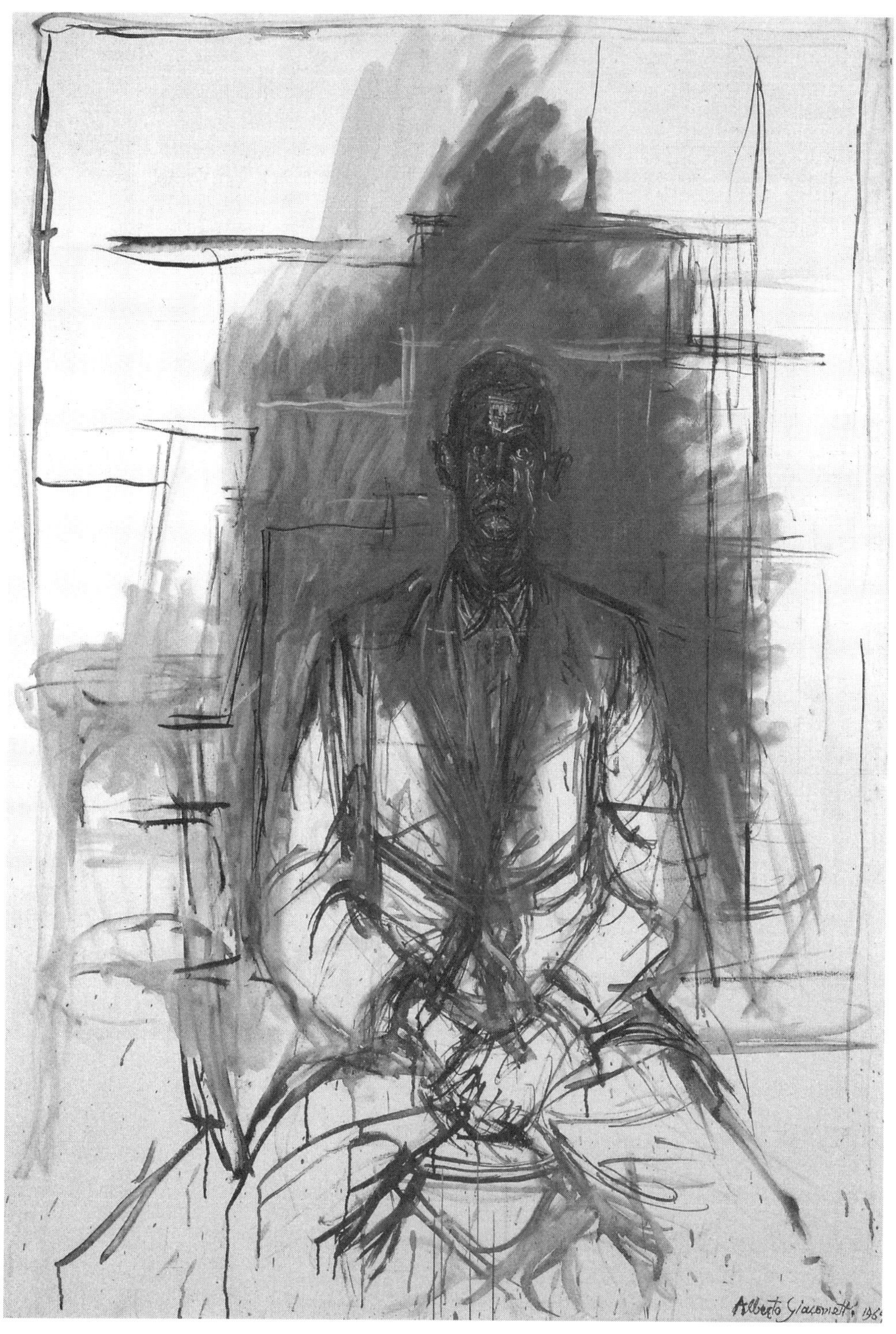
Alberto Giacometti

In the first place, there is a striking similarity between this painting and the drawing of 1954 to which I have given the number 3, the one that unites my likeness to that of Alberto. The pose is clearly reminiscent, but it is made to serve a very different conceptual purpose. The model's body does not serve here to situate the viewer at a specific distance. On the contrary, though the body is represented in detail, even including the forward movement of arms and legs and the arbitrary heightening of the torso, instead of situating the model in "realistic" perspective, as in the drawing, a reverse confrontation with the viewer is deliberately contrived in order to bring the head frontally forward as the most forthright element of the painting, leaving the rest of the figure virtually incidental. Another similarity to the drawing is the familiar use of overlapping, right-angled lines which serve no apparent representational purpose but set the model—in the painting, though not in the drawing—within a definitive spatial placement inside the "cloud" surrounding his head. This, of course, is enhanced by the obviously "unfinished" condition of the picture, which only adds to the forcefulness of the head as the center of the portrait's gravity, derived entirely from the lifelike dynamism of the model's gaze.

More and more it was the psychic significance of the human gaze that became the essential aspect of Giacometti's determination to translate, as it were, his visual experience into a vitally equivalent aesthetic image. He knew that this was impossible, for a painted canvas cannot live, but this very impossibility became a metaphysical objective to which the painter—and the sculptor—committed himself with intoxicating and despondent tenacity. Although he never failed to convey something of a likeness, Alberto saw that the reality of resemblance resides in a paradox, because no portrait actually embodies the appearance of a human being and consequently must be visualized as a generic image, beautiful and universal but personally abstract. A fossil bears the same relation in the burial of time to the original features of its long-ago life. Whenever I look at Alberto's painting of me, I perceive the emanation of a speculative likeness but not the rendered presence of a real resemblance, and yet I also perceive that this is a more vivifying depiction of human truth than any other portrait of myself, because a more profound search and commitment relating to truth went into it, and that, of course, is what Alberto sacrificed himself to impart.

By way of conclusion—though Alberto defies the very idea of conclusion—I may say that from the beginning I found the Giacometti portrait a very difficult, almost oppressive painting to live with. Alberto had—should I say, of course?—made me a gift of it. Thus, I hung it in my living room directly behind the couch where I have always been accustomed to sit. Others could see it, but I was not obliged to. When in solitude I did look at it, however, I recognized that this was a portrait of extraordinary power and intensity, a work which clearly appeared to have been devised for eternity, uncannily reminiscent of the purpose and effect of the Egyptian art which Giacometti admired more than any other, thus an image over which hovered the adumbration and presentiment of death, a prospect, incidentally, ever recurrent in the artist's conversation, a sinister omen, in fact, inasmuch as Alberto was to die only two years later and, moreover, expected to do so, having, as he readily acknowledged, done at age sixty-four everything necessary to leave his lifework all alone to live in his place.

MORGAN

One day in 1945 a Liberty ship of the U.S. Navy sailed into the Bay of Naples, bringing homeward a group of Italian prisoners of war. Among the American military men on board was a young fellow named Randall Morgan who spoke Italian and acted as an interpreter. Aged twenty-five, he came from a small town in Indiana. The sight of the world-famous bay that radiant morning became for him an epiphany which transformed his entire existence. Having returned temporarily to America to study art, he was back in Naples in 1948 and never again went home save for the occasional visit. The gemlike purity of the light, the limpid, azure Mediterranean, and the lovely, odorous wealth of vegetation which had captivated emperors, poets, and painters for two thousand years captivated Morgan. He settled on the Cape of Sorrento, where he was to live all the rest of his life and paint hundreds of pictures of the sea, of the luxuriant landscapes, and especially of enormous still lifes—flowers, fruit, vegetables, baskets, bowls, vases executed in magnified, painstaking detail against a cloudless sky. His work was from first to last ferociously representational in an era when abstraction ruled the art market and determined public taste. Nonetheless his paintings were regularly exhibited and found enough buyers to support the artist in modest comfort. But he never became well known, let alone famous, and this annoyed him.

I first met Randy, as all of his friends called him, during one of his, and my own, brief visits to New York. Then in 1958 I spent the summer with French friends on the southern escarpment of the cape in the little town of Positano, not yet devastated by the tourist armies. Randy happened to be there, too, director of a small but self-important art school which he was almost too clever to take seriously. Another American summering in Positano was the famous playwright Tennessee Williams whom I had met eleven years before during the Mardi Gras in New Orleans. Randy was eager to make the acquaintance of such a celebrity, and Tennessee, a lovely man despite his fame, took to newcomers with the gracious appreciation of a Southern gentleman-about-town. So the artist and the author got along very nicely, both being from small towns and less than ten years apart in age. After a couple of weeks Randy had the ingenious idea that it might be a fruitful thing if he were to make Tennessee's portrait, but he felt diffident about asking so recent an acquaintance to pose for him and wondered whether I might make the request. Tennessee was not only willing but also, I felt, ingenuously flattered. He wasn't the sort of man who would ever have assumed that by posing for his portrait he might magnify the artist's reputation.

Randy must have drawn and painted figure studies while in art school. He wouldn't have been approaching a portrait as if it were a novel challenge, but he had never personally applied himself to portraiture as a genre of any importance, and he never did. Yet he was

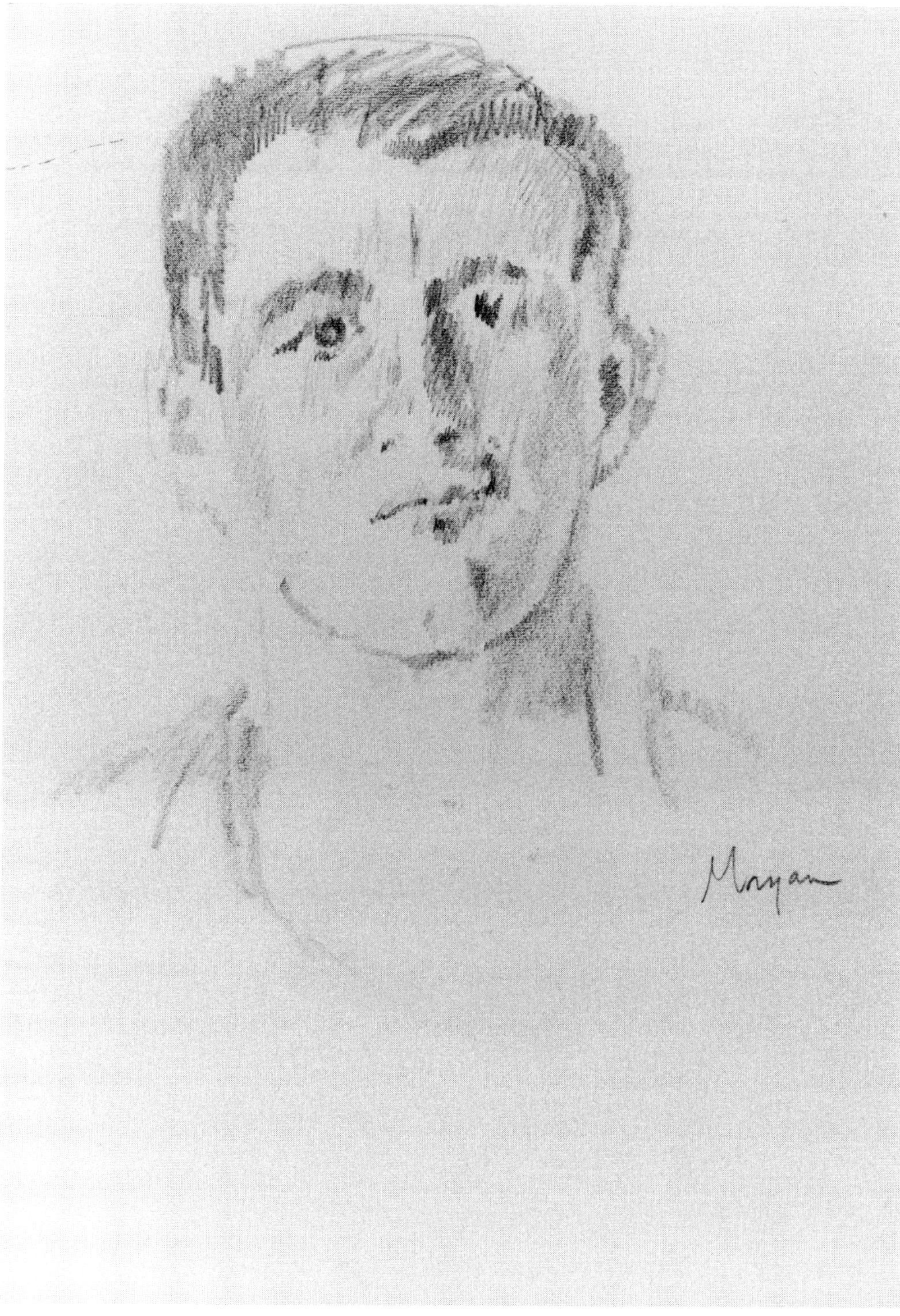

determined to portray his celebrated compatriot. Tennessee had to pose for three or four afternoons on Randy's terrace while the artist worked on a large drawing. The result was a very approximate likeness but rather a pretty drawing and, indeed, quite a flattering one, adding to Tennessee's somewhat malleable countenance a more forceful aspect of virility. The portrait was offered, of course, as a gift, and Tennessee carried it away with sincere smiles of appreciation. What became of it I have no idea, as I've never seen a reproduction, and the playwright was notoriously careless about possessions, changed his modest living quarters frequently, and was no admirer of his own countenance. Several years later he wrote a very poor play entitled *The Milk Train Doesn't Stop Here Anymore* based loosely on his stay in Positano, but there is no reference in it to Randy or to the author's portrait.

As a token, I suppose, of thanks for having facilitated the sitting of the playwright Randy proposed to draw my portrait, too. It was not nearly so large as the portrait of Tennessee, nor so flattering, nor so diligent an effort to capture a likeness. In fact, there is next to no likeness. Randy, I think, who was able to create in paint images of flowers and fruit of amazing accuracy, must have felt unsure of himself as a draftsman, but at the same time, he enjoyed the off-chance of producing a drawing now and then. And it is fair to say that my portrait has an exterior appeal purely as a drawing. There is something fresh and almost childlike about the features, while the quick, casual play of the pencil possesses an amiable charm. Though comparisons are rightfully belittled, it seems a curious coincidence that Randy's drawing of me rather resembles the draftsmanship of an Italian artist who devoted his lifetime to painting still lifes and almost nothing else: Giorgio Morandi, whose rare drawings are also fragile but charming. Morandi, of course, has received more posthumous recognition and fame than will ever be bestowed upon morose Randall Morgan, now also dead long since, but I am grateful to him for this would-be portrait which is so easy to contemplate with transient pleasure.

BALTHUS

By the mid-fifties, Balthus and I had become casual friends. This was Dora's doing. Though it would never have occurred to any of us that eventually he might draw my portrait, nevertheless one day he did. This, too, was Dora's doing. She liked to manipulate both personal and practical relations between her friends, and when it came to devising profitable transactions—for herself first of all and for others afterward—she was immune to embarrassment. Balthus by this time was installed in a ramshackle château in a very out-of-the-way corner of the French provinces. Having visited him there, we knew that furnishings, not to mention comforts, were few. It so happened that I had recently brought with me to Paris from my parents' attic in New Jersey an enormous Persian carpet which long ago had lain on the floor of my grandmother's living room in Indianapolis, Indiana. Being so large, it was of no imaginable use to me, but I'd spoken of its existence to Dora as the candid acknowledgment of an unduly acquisitive temperament, avoiding mention of my awareness that in this, at least, I was much like her. One evening in the spring of '57, at all events, while dining with Balthus in a modest restaurant called La Reine Christine, Dora remarked that I owned a splendid but outsized Persian carpet that I didn't know what to do with. And mightn't it be just the thing, she went on, to add a bit of warmth and elegance to the chilly, rather drab but vast salon of Balthus's château? "Perhaps," replied the artist with a supercilious shrug, but first, of course, he would have to inspect the merchandise and consider its price. Oh, said Dora promptly, smiling at me, she felt sure that James would not expect to receive cash money. That this was not plentiful in the painter's pockets was well known. A little sketch, a drawing or watercolor from the artist's hand would certainly do very well instead. I immediately concurred, and the artist, with another supercilious shrug, said, "Why not?" Seeing to his appreciation of the carpet was easily and quickly arranged. It was spread out on the sunlit lawn before the building where friends had amiably stored it. Balthus walked back and forth upon it, studied the color and weave and wear and finally said, "It will do." But I would have the responsibility of delivering it to the château. So the bargain was struck, and I felt quite satisfied by the prospect of possessing some little sketch by Balthus.

On April 3 I drove to Chassy, with the heavy and voluminous carpet occupying the entire rear seat of my small car. Balthus had begun to add insinuations of future grandeur to his bleak residence, and one of these was an Italian majordomo in a white jacket with gold buttons and epaulettes, bizarrely incongruous in that drab and impoverished valley. He was vigorously helpful, however, in bundling the weighty carpet into the house, where Balthus, his adolescent girlfriend, the servant, and I smoothed it out onto the chilly floor of the salon, where I thought it happily transformed the room by its antique rose and azure floral display. Striding across it, the

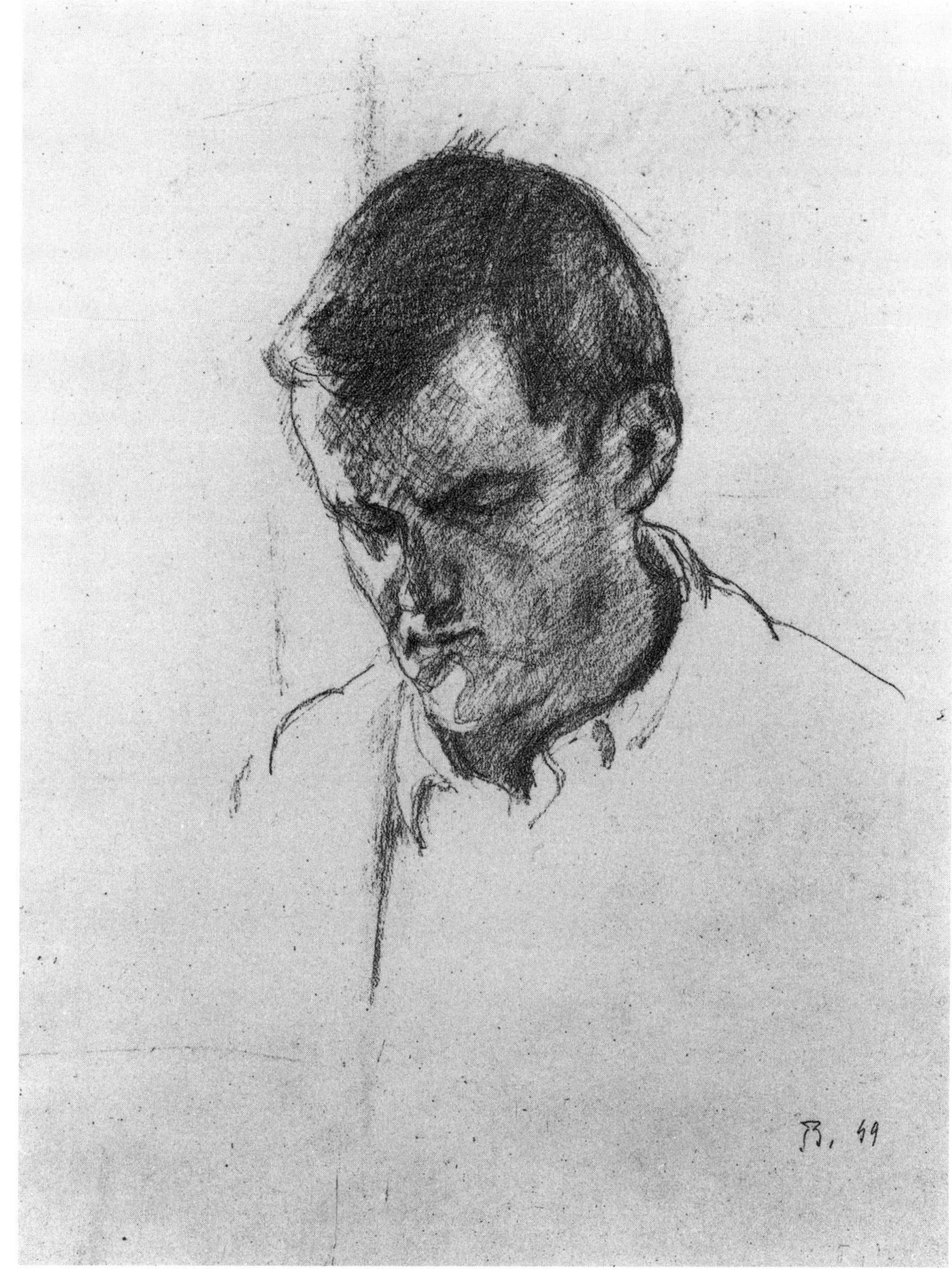

artist pronounced himself tolerably satisfied, and the girlfriend was plainly pleased by the addition of anything that would make the huge house more cheerful as a home. Having promptly kept my part of our bargain, I assumed that Balthus would be prepared to do likewise. How little I had as yet understood the perverse ways of the painter! He announced that we had barely time for a hurried tea before I would have to take again to the road for my return to Paris. I waited with rising surprise for mention of the little work from the artist's hand that had been promised. This came only at the last minute. Alas, said Balthus, escorting me to the door, he had no small sketches, watercolors, or suitable drawings which in all conscience he could offer in exchange. But by waiting, he assured me, I was losing nothing. A promise was a promise, and in time something good enough for me would assuredly come along. So I returned empty-handed and piqued to Paris. When I complained to Dora, she said that Balthus was an inveterate tease. He had given her a small painting ten years before but only recently after prolonged protestations had consented to sign it.* The artist was also a gentleman, however, and never would go back on his word. Therefore, indeed, I would lose nothing by waiting. So I waited. The weeks, months, and winter slipped by. Balthus appeared now and then in Paris. We had dinner with him. I felt shy about mentioning our bargain and believed, moreover, that it was up to the artist to keep his word without prompting. He referred occasionally to his promise, inevitably adding that I had nothing to lose by waiting. And I was prepared to

*Balthus, *Catalogue Raisonné de l'Oeuvre Complet* by Virginia Mounier and Jean Clair, Gallimard, Paris, 1999, page 145, No. 153.

wait, though it began to seem that I might be waiting for nothing. The thought was irritating, but I did not want to appear rude and grasping over anything so commonplace as a carpet.

A year had passed since its delivery. I decided to spend the spring around the lakes of northern Italy, visiting Venice in May and thereafter returning to Paris. Dora remarked that she had regretfully never visited La Serenissima and would be happy to join me there—paying her own way!—should this not be inconvenient. I was happy to agree. And then, she said, we could return via Milan, visit the Brera, travel on to Zurich and Basel, and drop in on Balthus at Chassy on the last stop of our homeward journey. This sounded altogether delightful, and it was. We arrived late at the artist's château, and he did not hide his annoyance at receiving guests in a dressing gown. But in the morning he was affable, insisting that we stay for lunch, served by the impeccable majordomo. And it was at the luncheon table that Dora showed her mettle as a friend and a diligent bargainer by remarking that I had as yet received no compensation for the fine carpet—in truth, it wasn't that good—which lay on the floor of the grand salon. Balthus predictably replied that I was losing nothing by waiting and that in the studio upstairs, anyway, there was not a single thing that would be suitable. Well, said Dora, that being the case, wouldn't it be simpler and more pleasing for all if Balthus were simply to make a portrait drawing of me? After all, I had already posed for Picasso, Alberto, Lucian, and herself. Not bad company to keep, said Balthus. So the understanding was reached. One carpet, one portrait. We drove back to Paris in the afternoon, both very pleased by this unexpected turn she had given to the original bargain.

That summer I spent on the Cape of Sorrento, hard at work on yet another unpublishable novel. In the autumn and winter I did quite a lot of traveling round Europe, passed the spring in a country house north of Paris, and the following summer in Greece. In between these absences I nonetheless saw something of friends in Paris, including occasionally Balthus, and no mention was made of the aleatory portrait. Returning to Paris toward the end of September, I made plans to fly to America six weeks later to spend a few months with my family in New Jersey and friends in New York. Two and a half years had now passed since delivery of Granny's carpet to Chassy, eighteen months since the promise of a portrait in exchange. I began to suspect that Balthus's incentive to tease was in fact a source of gratification gained by gratuitously tantalizing persons less self-confident, and this suspicion, moreover, seemed to go nicely along with the artist's recent insistence that he receive the deference due an authentic nobleman, as he was entitled to the hereditary rank of count passed down from illustrious Polish forebears. It was a ludicrous affectation, of course, derided loudly behind his back, and by no one more sincerely than his elder brother, though people took care not to smirk in his presence. At all events, I felt that a promise freely given is a debt honorably contracted, and that I was being hoodwinked, which rankled. When I complained to Dora, she suggested that I deliver an ultimatum, a tactic, she said, which had often worked well with Picasso when he turned guileful.

So I sat down on October 10th, Alberto's birthday, and wrote Balthus a letter—he had no telephone—stating my case politely but stipulating that unless he could contrive to keep his promise before my return to the United States on November 12th, I would come to

Chassy and take back the carpet. The following Tuesday, three days later, I received a telegram reading, "EXPECT YOU THURSDAY. FRIENDLY REGARDS. BALTHUS." I felt pleasantly vindicated, and set off Thursday morning with complacent satisfaction under a radiant sky, arriving just in time for tea. It was served by the majordomo in the grand salon, now, indeed, having acquired approximate grandeur by addition not only of a suitable carpet but also a grand piano, some Louis XVI side chairs, luxurious yellow draperies, couches, and armchairs provided by the Parisian decorator Henri Samuel in exchange for a couple of splendid paintings. Hardly had he gulped a cup of Earl Grey before the artist leapt up and said that I knew where I'd be sleeping and he would expect to see me later for drinks, say seven-thirty. We had some champagne at that hour, then an excellent dinner in the adjoining dining room, chatted about Alberto and Annette, Picasso and Dora, Arezzo, Seurat, Signorelli, concluding with the imperious recommendation that the next day I should drive to Autun, only about fifty miles away, to admire the incomparable tympanum of the cathedral. Nor should I miss the museum and its lovely nativity by the Master of Flemalle. Then there was a very pleasant restaurant called Le Vieux Moulin where I could have lunch out of doors beside a pretty stream. I'd be back at Chassy just in time for a bath, drinks, and dinner. No mention of a portrait. Now, I had already told Balthus that I must leave on Saturday afternoon, no later than four o'clock, having promised to dine with Marie-Laure de Noailles, an engagement he would be the first to acknowledge as unbreakable, since she was not only a genuine viscountess but also had been the model for what was probably his finest portrait.

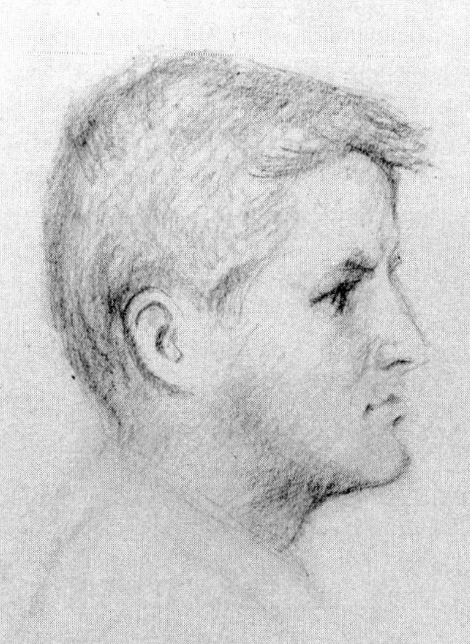

So I went to Autun, admired the tympanum, the fine Flemish paintings, had an excellent lunch, and drove back to Chassy beside glittering streams and ruined sawmills. That evening at dinner, having waited twenty-four hours without mention of the purpose of my visit, I made bold with an inquiry as to when I might expect to be portrayed. The artist threw up his hands, exclaiming that psychological readiness for the ordeal of a portrait was so essential that, although a drawing might take a few minutes, the mental stress of preparation might in some cases last nearly a lifetime. It sounded like Alberto talking, and I suspected that the tease was working to elaborate effect. Moreover, Balthus certainly realized that I would never make good my threat to carry away the carpet. Anyway, he added, we had all day Saturday before us. I reminded him that I must leave at the very latest by four in the afternoon. Well, he rejoined with a sly smile, nobody need worry because the creative disposition could sometimes make a quarter of an hour virtually equivalent to a lifetime. Then the dinner was over, and Balthus bid me a courtly good night, followed dutifully upstairs by his current nymphet, named Frédérique. It was no surprise to find on the bookshelf in my room the covert first edition of *Lolita*.

In the morning Balthus had come and gone at the breakfast table before I reached it. He was in his studio, I was informed, and under no circumstances to be disturbed. I packed my small suitcase, then waited in the salon. Balthus's studio was immediately overhead. I could hear his footsteps as he paced back and forth, presumably judging a painting in progress between every few strokes of the brush. The weather again was gorgeous. Shafts of pure October gold poured through the high windows. How long I waited I didn't watch. Too long. All the morning. It seemed, in any case, far longer than the best frame of mind in the world would have cared to consider urbane, not to mention well-bred, and my frame of mind was by no means of the best.

It was well past noon, anyway, when Balthus finally came downstairs. He brought with him, though, a large sketchbook and a handful of pencils. This seemed a promising sign, and it was, for he languidly remarked, "Well, now, my dear Jim, we shall have our little session of posing, shall we not?" And if the psychic strain of preparation had been an ordeal, he showed no sign of it. "Just sit in that armchair and face me. Good. Like that. And lower your head."

He sat in a chair facing me, opened the sketchbook on his knees, and began to draw, studying his model carefully from minute to minute. Alberto having accustomed me to lengthy sessions of absolute immobility, I had no difficulty holding the pose. The work took fifteen or twenty minutes, no more, and appeared to come easily. Balthus announced that the drawing was finished and tore the page from his sketchbook.

From the very first instant that I saw the drawing, I disliked it. I saw in it next to nothing of myself. And the drawing, I felt, saw of myself even less than I did. The face being bent forward, the eyes are so cast down that they appear to be shut, as if the model had been asleep, asleep perchance in that ultimate slumber from which there is no awakening, and thus deprived forever of metaphysical being. The head is motionless, compact, like a stone sculpture which the artist has chosen to interpret for abstract practice of skillful draftsmanship. The lips, compressed, convey no sense of breath or feeling. From a purely formal point of view the drawing is powerful but awkward due to the skewed and overemphasized highlights beneath the mouth, the right nostril, and eye. All in all, likeness left to indifference, the drawing is no portrait but a roughly executed representation of a male head, looking very like that of an anonymous ruffian or, perhaps, a man recently released from prison. If this were the product of Balthus's inclination to tease, and to use creative originality to express a lack of esteem, then I thought he'd done well. I was naïve, not nearly astute enough to realize that a young fellow from the uncultivated continent of North America should never have presumed to call to account over a mere rug an artist and nobleman from the heartland of ancient Europe. But then . . . the world at large had a lot to learn about Balthus. A bargain, however, remained justly a bargain, so I said that the drawing was fine and the portrait excellent, both compliments backhanded, in which Balthus nonetheless acquiesced with his sly smile, placing the page on the closed lid of the grand piano, and then the majordomo ceremoniously proclaimed that the count's luncheon awaited.

Coffee was served in the salon in tiny transparent cups decorated with golden crowns and amber bumblebees which had belonged, Balthus remarked, to his great-grandmother. I said that I must be on my way, not wishing to keep Marie-Laure waiting. "No, no," cried Balthus, "the afternoon's barely begun. I must make another drawing, a profile this time. Take your seat, Jim."

Assuming the artist wanted a souvenir for himself, I sat again in the armchair, while Balthus moved to one side, the sketchbook in his lap. The second drawing required appreciably less work and concentration than the first, and when it was presently torn from the sketchbook and passed across to me, I immediately recognized why.

It was, it is, a work of ineffable delicacy and finesse, an image which defies the viewer to discern where the artist's visual volition has ceased to direct his hand and art itself as an ontological first cause has determined the aesthetic effect. A work, in short, so definitive that as a drawing it can be defined only by reference to itself. As a portrait it pulses with a palpable life all its own, imbued with the mysterious tenderness which emanates from Balthus's finest paintings. As a likeness I like to imagine that the artist actually saw the resemblance which endures on the page, but one may wonder whether he didn't mean to please by making me more handsome than reality had, and that would presumably have been the artist's private pleasure. Though the right eye alone is visible, it gazes with perceptive vitality to the inward and outward horizon, fixed upon an immensity of richest expectation. Thus, art had demonstrated yet again that art does see beyond the horizon of the human brain. The moment of appreciation was transcendent and it goes without saying that I couldn't understand what had happened to the creative vision between the first drawing and the second. Something decisive. But in the artist or in the model? Or in the symbiosis which unites them in the creation of a reality to which both have given more than either can contrive to understand? And yet nothing made by mankind means so much.

Balthus took the drawing from my hands and placed it on the lid of the grand piano. I stood up.

"Sit down, Jim," he said. "Now that I've got my hand in I don't want to let another glimpse slip by."

I obediently resumed the pose without further prompting, while Balthus slid his own chair slightly backward.

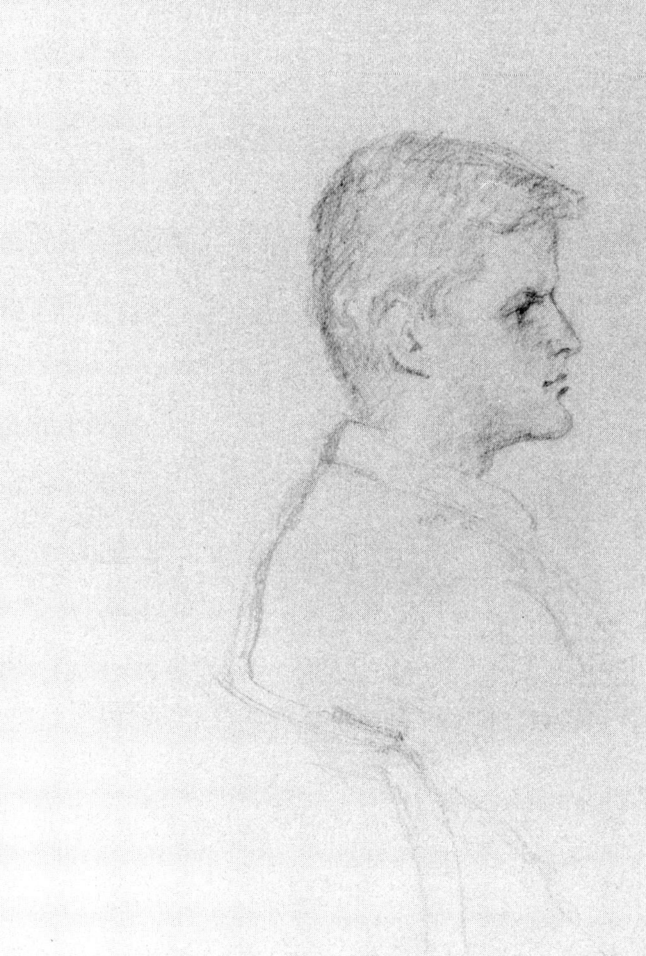

The third portrait may be considered the best, because it fills the page with more detail, seeming more complex and balanced, more "finished," as it were, in the style of a traditional portrait, since my jacket and right shoulder and the back of my chair are lightly indicated to fill the space below the head. This dominates, of course, though it is somewhat smaller than its predecessor, having been viewed from farther away. But the two profiles are so similar as to be almost identical in every detail save size, and consequently all the admiration and the wonder that I tried to summon by surmise in pondering upon the second portrait, the head alone, might reasonably appear apposite in contemplation of the third. Certainly, yes. And yet . . . the very "finish" of the third drawing seems to diminish its intensity as a clairvoyant human image when set beside the incomparable rendition of the head alone. Not every comparison, after all, is ineffectual. Many, indeed, like this one, disclose the enigmatic power of art to offer to everyone who looks for it a more profound and emancipated revelation of his transient significance. Balthus admired Alberto more than any other artist of his century, and Alberto often remarked that a profile could not be a satisfactory portrait because it inevitably lacked the life of the model's gaze. But I believe that Balthus's drawing of my profile, my head alone, would have roused Alberto's astonishment and admiration by bringing to life not only what is visible but also what is unseen though at the same time a vital element of the entire aesthetic experience. To say that such an accomplishment illustrates an ability surpassing the confines of talent is to say how mean are mere words when confronted by a tangible illustration of how some lives survive decease.

Balthus took the third sheet and placed it alongside the others on the lid of the piano. As I studied all three I felt befuddled, longing to ask whether I might select the drawing of my choice to complete our bargain but knowing that courtesy dictated acceptance of the first. While I hesitated Balthus signed each one in the lower right hand corner with his initial and the date " '59." Knowing I would never have another opportunity to be indiscreet, having already been impertinent, I mumbled something to the effect of wondering whether I might choose the one I liked most in order to fulfill our agreement.

"Not at all, my dear Jim," Balthus exclaimed. "You must have all three."

"But our understanding was for one," I protested. "One portrait for one carpet. I'd feel embarrassed to take more."

"I insist," said the artist. "You came all this way to pose for me, and I've very, very rarely done drawings of men. So it's really I who owe you a favor. You must take all three and be on your way, not keep Marie-Laure waiting." I must truthfully acknowledge that he did not have to insist very strenuously to secure my agreement. So we rolled up the three drawings and went out to the car. Frédérique came along to wave me on my way. That was the last time I saw the Château de Chassy, but the artist has remained very present for me till now. Nor do I expect him ever to be absent.

As I drove back to Paris I couldn't help wondering what creative cleavage had taken place between the execution of the first perplexing, problematic drawing before lunch and the two beautiful, remarkable ones afterward. It no longer seemed reasonable to assume that the first had been done deliberately to tease, however perverse the artist was known to be. Yet on the evidence of the two later drawings the first could not have been the purposeful pursuit of a likeness. Then it was a record, I thought, of Balthus revealing something to himself via my presence but not by means of my appearance. I imagine it must have had something to do with his concept of the artist as a being set apart from others in the fretful solitude and splendor of his vocation. And later, perhaps, by way of radical contrast befitting a courteous nobleman, the true vision of imperious creative conscience brought forth the very best he could do. The three drawings, in any case, tell a strange and admirable story about a man who, like all true artists, left the world without revealing what it was that had enabled him so mysteriously to enrich it.

MASON

One afternoon in November 1968, I wandered into the gallery of Pierre Matisse in New York and there came upon an exhibition of representational figures which moved me more forcefully than any works of sculpture I'd seen since Giacometti's death two years before. They did not in the least resemble works by Alberto but were powerful in a highly original style which I thought would have impressed him. Also on view were drawings in India ink of similar strength and assurance. Altogether it was an exhibition of truly exceptional creative vitality, and I was quick to tell Pierre how profoundly this work impressed me. The artist, I learned, was Raymond Mason, an Englishman who had been living and working in Paris by that time for nearly twenty years. Needless and sad to say, Mason's exhibition did not excite the New York art world, then already mired in the morass of fashionable trash in which it remains complacently immersed to this day. In any case, I felt at once that it would be richly rewarding to make the acquaintance of this artist. Pierre graciously paved the way, and less than a month later I was knocking on a door at the rear of a decrepit courtyard at number 60 rue Monsieur-le-Prince, not far from the Luxembourg Gardens.

Tall and stalwart, with a craggy face and rumbling voice, Mason has changed amazingly little in thirty-odd years. When we met he was at work on a very large sculpture in deep relief depicting a scene in the central market of Paris with a dozen figures, every sort of fruit or vegetable, and dominated by the looming silhouette of the Saint-Eustache Church. It is an amazing and unique creation, with roots in the late Middle Ages, the London of Hogarth and Gin Lane, and the Paris of Honoré Daumier. I was amazed by its daring. Raymond and I became friends in five minutes. In a month I was welcomed for dinner with embarrassing regularity by Raymond's Eurasian wife, Janine, and their two young daughters. When the market sculpture was exhibited in a well-known gallery, I wrote for an art review called *L'Oeil* an article in praise of it and of Raymond's oeuvre altogether.

The Masons owned a charming, tumbledown ruin of a house in Provence near Ménerbes, where I had long before spent happy days with Dora. From the terrace there overlooking a verdant, unspoiled valley and striated mountainsides in the distance Raymond made many fine drawings and watercolors, being as skilled with a sable brush as with a reed pen. Late in August of 1972 I spent several days at Ménerbes with the Masons. In the stark southern sunlight one afternoon on the terrace Raymond asked me to hold the pose while he painted a watercolor portrait in profile.

Like everything else made by Mason, this portrait could not imaginably have been executed by anyone else. It is, in the first place, unmistakably the work of a sculptor and situates itself stylistically in time as a product of the late twentieth century. That it should be reproduced in black and white is somewhat regrettable,

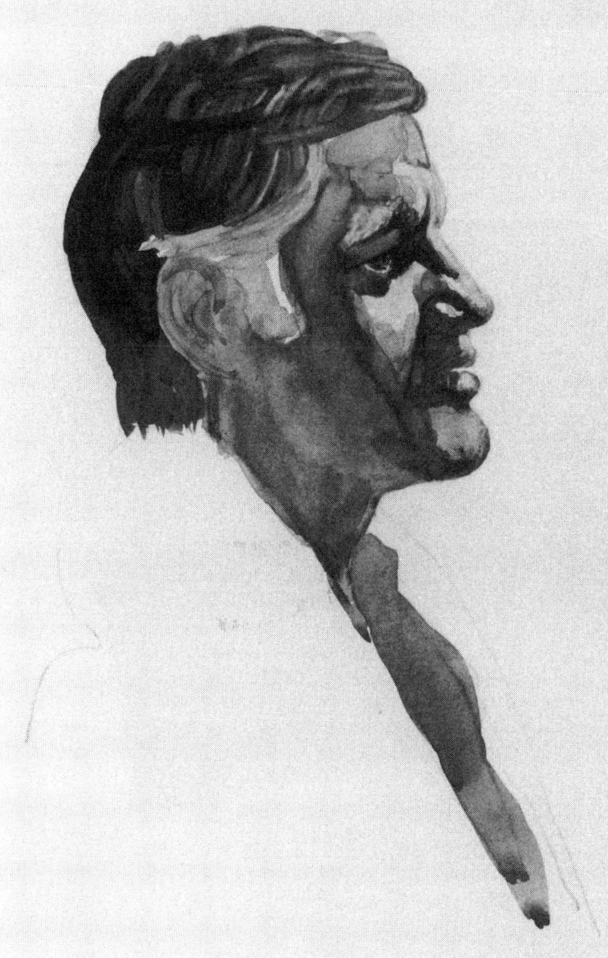
Raymond Mason '72

because the juxtaposition of color planes emphasizes a decidedly sculptural expression in the configuration of the head and its formal features. And it is precisely this sculptural character which constitutes the remarkable representational animation of the portrait, for it imparts to a profile the uncanny impression of a visage fully perceived in the round, though in appearance it also imparts, perhaps, a semblance of aggressiveness: the forward thrust of jaw, full and parted lips, assertive nose, and sly eye may have been seen as suggestive of pugnacity. Above all there arises from the page a startling sense of lived life, its unsparing emotions, stoical dreams, and arduous tasks. Thus, it is not an image from which a model might ever derive narcissistic gratification. As a likeness it is deeply personal on both sides of the work of art.

A couple of years after Raymond painted this portrait Pierre Matisse organized yet another exhibition of his work, painted landscape bas-reliefs and watercolors of the Provençal countryside near his home. I was asked to compose a preface for the catalogue. By way of conclusion I wrote, "To see is to look, to watch, to visualize, to understand, to recognize, to judge, to know. These imperative capacities constitute the passion of the artist. He is a seer, but he is also the most pragmatic of realists. Wresting from space its physical and symbolic structure, he compels us to participate in the passionate use of his life by his eye. He offers us a glorious opportunity to see that we see, and in vision to perceive what may redeem from transience and squalor our brief experience of the world."

CARTIER-BRESSON

My first meeting with Henri Cartier-Bresson took place after a lengthy, indecisive, almost whimsical telephone conversation between us had finally led me to the lobby of the Hôtel Regina at precisely 11:30 a.m. on the eighteenth of May, 1970. I had solicited the meeting in order to talk about Giacometti in the hope of gaining further information for the sculptor's biography, as the two men had been friends for many years. We went for a stroll in the Tuileries Gardens. Cartier-Bresson told me that everything revealing that he might say about Alberto had been best expressed in the numerous photographs he had made of the artist, for whom he had always felt limitless admiration. To be sure, many of the photographs of Giacometti, not only by Cartier-Bresson but by numerous others, such as Brassaï and Man Ray, are expressive and eloquent, yet despite the popular adage half a dozen discerning words can tell more than a photograph can. So I was rather disappointed by the failure to obtain information of any value about Alberto, though Cartier-Bresson may have thought to compensate by bitterly condemning the grasping and malicious conduct of the artist's widow, about all of which I knew only too much already. He concluded, however, by inviting me to lunch with his recently wed second wife, a woman far younger than he, also a photographer, attractive and sophisticated, named Martine Franck.

Thereafter I ran into them here and there at exhibition openings and parties at the homes of mutual friends. They invited me to dinner in a newly installed apartment overlooking the Tuileries and half the city. I returned the invitation. Their company was cultivated and stimulating. We became friends. One evening at the house of Raymond and Janine Mason while Henri and I were chatting in a corner of the salon he suddenly declared that he would like me to pose for one of his photoportraits, as he called them. At the time, and still today, I suppose, he was widely acknowledged to be the most celebrated but also the most accomplished photographer living, committed to a level of vision high above photojournalism, an artist to whom truth and integrity were paramount. His models had included scores of great artists, writers, musicians, scientists, and statesmen, as well as countless anonymous people viewed with exceptional acuity and compassion—lovers, prisoners, pimps, prostitutes, children, princes and paupers, the wretched and outcast, a vast panorama of mankind. The critics revered him as a master, compared his art to the writings of Balzac and Kafka, and considered his photoportraits metaphysical images in which the models seem to have received the revelation of their destiny. Be all this as it may, I was by no means averse to posing for Henri. Indeed, I greeted the proposal with elation, supposing, perhaps, that his camera might work some sorely needed magic for my very mediocre destiny.

So we set a date for the session. It was a Saturday, the twenty-first of February, 1976, at three in the afternoon. The sky outside

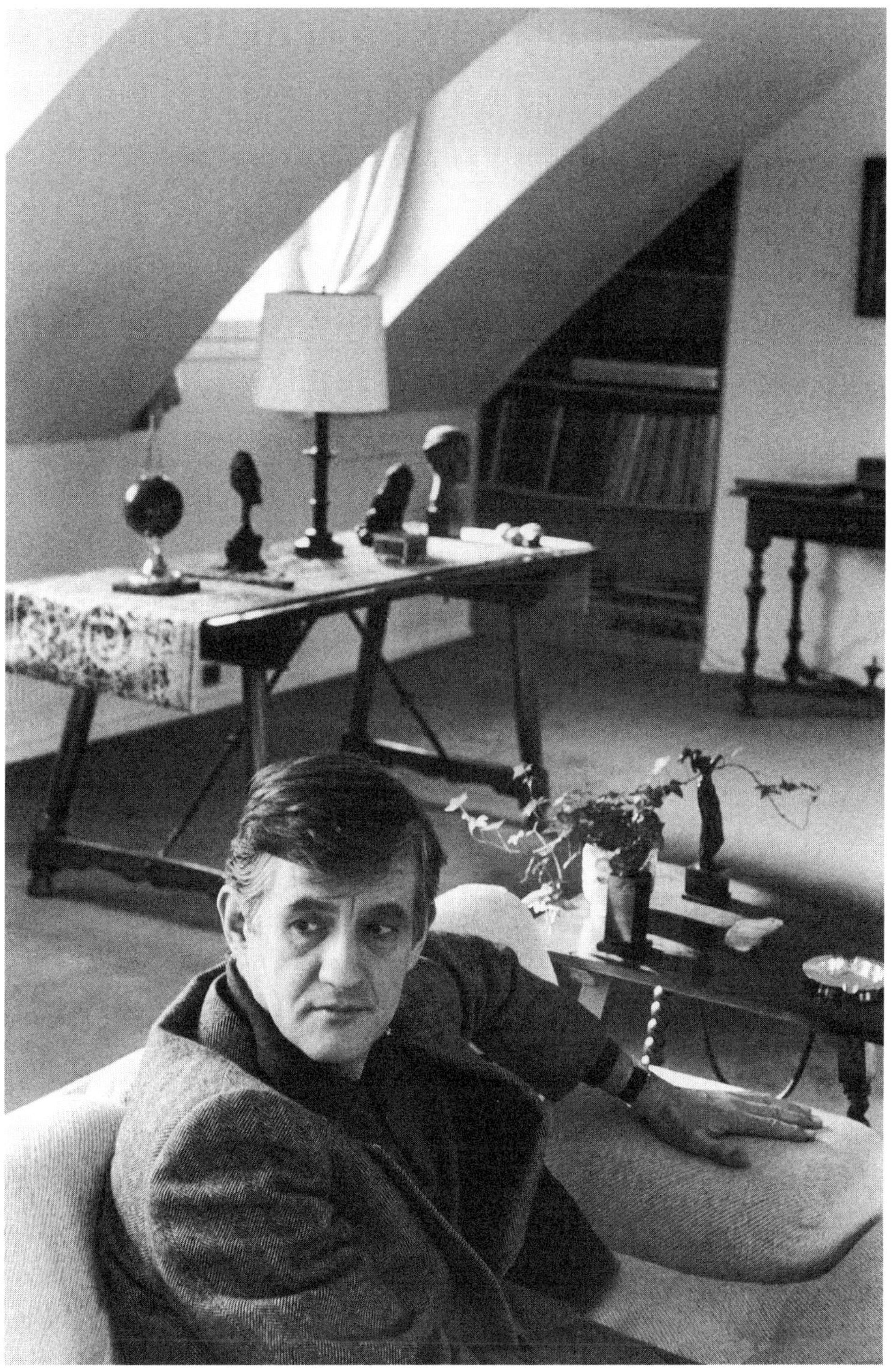

was gray, but that didn't appear to concern Henri. "To take photographs," he once said, "means to recognize—simultaneously within a fraction of a second—both the fact itself and the rigorous organization of visually perceived forms that give it meaning. It is putting one's head, one's eye, and one's heart on the same axis." This, of course, is wishful rhetoric. To "recognize" so much in an instant is possible only for a machine, which, to be sure, is what a camera is, and it, alas, possesses no head, no eye, and definitely no heart. A human viewer possesses all three, and many of Henri's photographs are powerfully moving by virtue of what degree of cultivated awareness one is able to bring to them. The photographer, however, is at the mercy, so to speak, of his machine. Henri has entitled one of his volumes of photographs *The Decisive Moment*. The decision is made by the camera. It becomes momentous *after* the fact, not before, according to the aesthetic discretion of the photographer, who selects the decisive image from amongst an indeterminate quantity of negatives. There is no getting round the vital gap between what the mind thinks it sees and what the eye actually perceives, and it is this impassable gap which forever differentiates the static fixity of a photographic image from the tremulous mutability of a work of art, which from century to century, if not from hour to hour, is never the same.

Henri's approach in the hunt for a portrait was casually stealthy. He asked me to sit down at the end of a couch and move about as if alone in search of a comfortable position. As I did so he silently circled round, snapping his camera repeatedly until the film was finished. This took no more than ten minutes. "I think I've got something," he said, "but I'll have to go over the contact sheets to find it." What he found is the photograph reproduced here. He felt that it was a valid portrait. It is a petrified likeness, certainly, and if one isolates the face from the background there appears a resemblance to a portrait and superimposed upon it a resemblance to a person, a resemblance, however, so unsparingly and ineluctably detailed that the subject's persona is overwhelmed by the very multiplicity of detail, while a viewer's perceptive faculties are thwarted by the generic similitude of the model's features to those of all mankind. The greatest portraitists, even van Eyck, never allowed themselves to be dominated by physiognomic detail. In short, the photographed face of James Lord becomes a prototype. To say that it is an image in which the model seems to have received the revelation of his destiny is nonsense. If, on the other hand, one conceals the face, observing only the background and assuming it to be the house of the seated individual, one may make many assumptions about his personality and character. The three tables, their placement, and the objects upon them all have more to reveal about him than his features, and as for his destiny the unmistakable sculpture by Alberto Giacometti on the Spanish table should, indeed, be a revelation. A man's home is made in the image of his temperament. As photographs go—and it is obvious I don't believe they go very far—the one which Henri selected as the best among thirty-six is a pleasing memento of myself at age fifty-three. The photographer himself, however, would have been the first to see incomparably less in it than in a drawing by Alberto or Balthus. It was just at this moment, indeed, that Henri turned decisively away from photography after a lifetime as "the greatest photographer of modern times."

As a young man Henri had aspired to become a painter and studied with a third-rate fellow traveler of cubism by the name of André Lhote. It turned out that nobody, and least of all himself, judged his early creative efforts sufficiently gifted to promise much distinction for an artistic career. Being financially independent—a fact which he has all his life been at pains to conceal—the young fellow set off on travels across the world, taking along a camera to record whatever attracted the sensitive and passionate response of an already disciplined eye. Many of these photographs reverberate with a striking sense of historical and anthropological perception. They made his name and fame before the age of forty, when consecration was bestowed by an exhibition at the Museum of Modern Art in New York. Thereafter he proceeded from success to success as a photographer artist.

Then at the age of sixty-six, when most men accost the emancipation of retirement, Cartier-Bresson audaciously set aside the fulfillment and acumen of judicious maturity in favor of the unsatisfied aspirations of youth. Had he always been dogged, perhaps, by the qualm that photography could not produce art? I suspect so. Now, in any case, he put away his camera and applied himself to pencil and paper. Common sense would have advised that an eye dedicated for forty years to the technique of a machine cannot revert overnight to the pristine vision of boyhood. But the bondage of creativity is not sensible. Henri applied himself to drawing with innocent tenacity. Though he sought advice from a couple of artist friends who knew too well the complexities of draftsmanship to believe that advice could help, Henri never applied himself to rigorous formal training. And maybe, all in all, this was just as well. But he devoted himself to his inflexible task with unsparing perseverance.

The results were mediocre and amateurish but by this very character imbued with the originality, so to speak, of inexperienced and studious scrutiny. The subject matter was varied: landscapes, interiors, architecture, portraits, even portraits of himself, he who had fiercely refused ever to be photographed. As I was fairly often on hand, Henri pressed me into service as a model. He didn't have to press very hard, because by this time I was not only accustomed to posing but derived from the experience a peculiar tingle of gratification, as if by relinquishing my person to the artist's use I was liable to discover a self hitherto inscrutable. This did not often occur, but the possibility remained provocative. The quality of the portrait was irrelevant. In Henri's case this was to the good. He apologized for not making me a gift of one of the sketches for which I posed, explaining that all of his drawings without exception were set aside for his daughter and that never under any circumstances might he consent to part with a single one. That was quite all right with me. He and Martine had been unable to have children and therefore had adopted a little girl whom they named Melanie, an odd choice since it means blackness and the child had the complexion of a magnolia.

It was outlandishly inconsistent with Henri's determination to appear in modest circumstances that the Cartier-Bressons owned a fine house and extensive property on the outskirts of a quiet Provençal town called Céreste. Maybe, however, the estate had been a gift from Martine's father, reputed to be the richest man in Belgium, owner of an oceangoing yacht (which Henri hated) and an outstanding collection of paintings, including masterpieces by van Gogh and Cézanne. I was invited on several occasions to visit them in the Midi. Henri and I went for long hikes in the back country, talked candidly of our lives, and took naps in the fragrant meadows. And it was in the large living room at Céreste that I posed on the Fourth of July, 1978, for the portrait reproduced here. It is, as I recall the most "finished" of all those that Henri made of me. There is no need to describe its failure as a portrait or its defects of draftsmanship. A studied glance is enough to tell the regrettable story of a mistaken vocation. What may be of anecdotal interest, though, is how this drawing happened to come into my possession despite the artist's resolve to preserve for Melanie every work of art to come from his hand.

In the Parisian art world it was no secret that Henri had for some years been expending his energies exclusively on drawings. People were curious to see what they looked like, and the Cartier-Bresson name was certain to attract crowds. Consequently the Museum of Modern Art of the City of Paris set about preparing an exhibition of Henri's drawings with the artist's reticent but elated cooperation. This was to be shown during 1981 and a catalogue was in preparation. No secret, either, was the fact that for some twenty years I had regularly produced critical articles and catalogue prefaces devoted to the work of artists I admired, most prominent among them being Alberto Giacometti, who happened also to be the artist and man most seriously esteemed by Cartier-Bresson, whose many photographs of Alberto were famous evidence of admiration. So it came about as a fateful ordination, I suppose, that Henri asked me to write the preface to the catalogue for his exhibition. Now, Henri in the past had been generous with gifts of his photographs not only to me but also to my friend and adopted son, Gilles, whom he had photographed during a visit to Céreste, and in addition I was truly fond of both him and his wife, considered them faithful, trustworthy friends, and contemplated with reluctance the refusal of what must have seemed to them a normal and complimentary proposal. It was with prudent reluctance, however, that I considered the compromise of consent. And yet common decency, if not common sense, argued forcefully for it. So I said yes.

In writing my preface I determined insofar as possible to say nothing I did not believe to be true about Henri's drawings themselves and his pursuit of honest draftsmanship. This was far from easy, but with the careful camouflage of florid rhetoric I came tolerably close to my intention while seeming to assert that Henri's drawings deserved discerning appreciation. The artist's preconception of praise was quite adequately satisfied. I was embarrassed but not ashamed, and our friendship ripened on the branch of his esteem.

Three years later it all went wrong. A large retrospective exhibition of works by Balthus was shown in Paris at the Centre Pompidou during the last months of 1983, then in New York at the Metropolitan Museum early in 1984. I was invited to write a critical article on the artist by the editor of a review of arts and letters at that time influential, and the article appeared in December 1983. I wrote frankly, not neglecting the eccentric aristocratic pretensions of the artist but also expressing sincere admiration for his large symbolic paintings, which may well deserve consideration as masterpieces. To my astonishment, this article stirred up a hurricane of indignation in the volatile teacup of the international art world, where my comments on the count's affectation were interpreted as

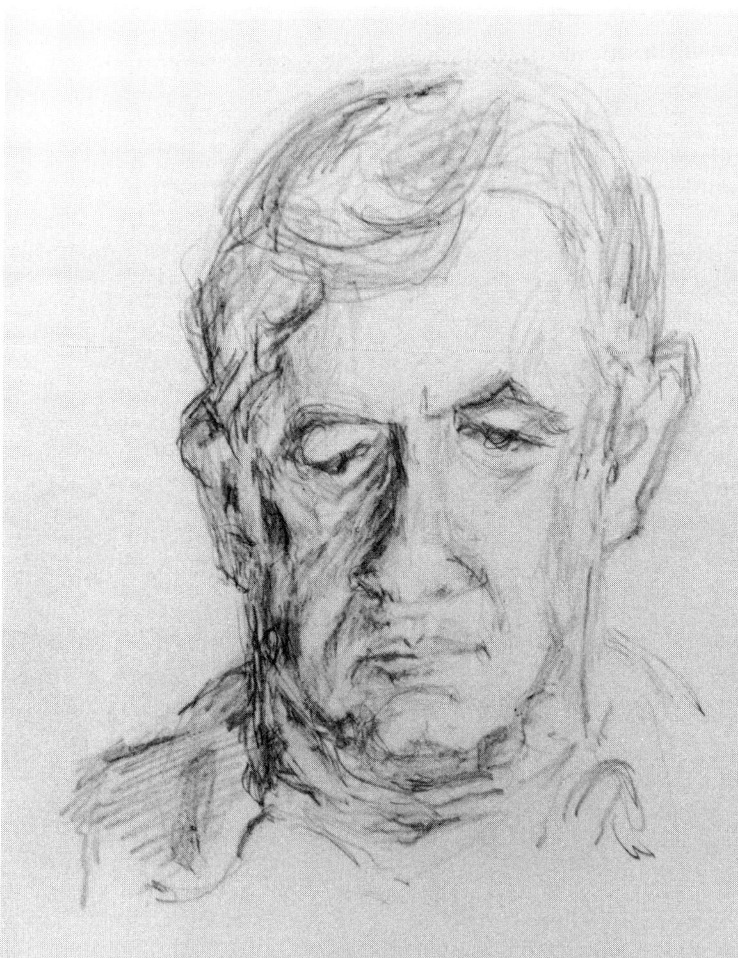
H.C.B
7.78

scurrilous slander. I thought all this ridiculous, but there were those who decidedly didn't and Henri was one of them. News of estrangement travels fast, especially in creative circles, where it can become bitter overnight. I didn't understand Henri's reasons or motives, but hearing nothing from him I did not feel it was up to me to seek reconciliation. Henri, after all, had always been a fierce advocate of the truth, and he knew just as much about Balthus's idiosyncrasies as I had written, and probably more. They didn't bother him, I suspected, but publication evidently did. We ran into each other one day at an exhibition. He was courteous but distant. I took the opportunity to express my puzzlement at his reaction. He replied that he could explain it and suggested that we have lunch together en tête-à-tête for him to do this. So we had lunch in a false aura of former friendliness. We talked about trivialities while I attempted repeatedly to turn the conversation toward Balthus or at least around the quandary of an intimacy incomprehensibly corroded. To no avail. It was not that Henri was evasive or disingenuous. He seemed simply to be unaware of what I endeavored to discuss or, indeed, of what had brought us face-to-face. He was, as always, irreproachably courteous but apparently at a total loss to grasp the reason for our meeting. And presently I was at no less of a loss myself. When we parted, it was with the absurd intimation on Henri's part that we would doubtless meet soon again on similarly amicable terms. Of course we never did. The aimless, almost incoherent conversation of that day was our last. When accidental encounters occurred at exhibitions, a few polite banalities were the best either could contrive.

Then I learned that our estrangement was less than ever matter for a baffled smile. The biography of Alberto Giacometti at which I had labored for fifteen years was finally published in New York. Thinking to be sporting, I sent a copy to Alberto's old friend Henri. I received no thanks. Word soon enough came my way that Henri disapproved of the biography. This time I was not only perplexed but indignant. How could the uncompromising apostle of truth find fault with an account of his friend's life which he could not have failed to recognize as punctiliously faithful to fact, of which, indeed, the sculptor's own brother later said (for publication), "Without the profound understanding which united Alberto Giacometti and James Lord this biography would not have been so exact." This time, though, I found an inkling of what might so trouble Henri that friendship became of no account and care for the truth ineffectual. During our long rambles through the Provençal countryside Henri had reminisced with ingenuous zest about his personal past, his romances, adventures, and companions. Thus, I learned much about his life and observed with fond amusement the adolescent fads and mannerisms which he cherished fifty years later. Having seen with what candor I wrote about Balthus and Alberto, I suspected he must be afraid I might do likewise concerning him, and of this I knew he would be intemperately fearful, aware of his own fierce aversion to the sort of intimate revelation that he sought to portray in photographs of his models. If, indeed, he worried, it was a waste of feeling. I never considered Henri a promising subject for meaningful biography. In the first place, he nourished the ridiculous conviction that biography was morbid, and in the second he was personally far too secretive and fickle.

Meanwhile, his exhibition of drawings made its prestigious way across the world, from Paris to Mexico, to Sweden, to Italy, England,

Austria, Greece, America, Japan, Spain, and in several of those venues my original preface of 1981 appeared in the catalogue, permission to republish having properly been requested in advance, though never by Henri in person, always by curators of the various museums. But I never refused.

My astonishment consequently was appreciable when early in 1996 I received a letter from the proprietor of a commercial gallery in London advising me that he was preparing an exhibition for the sale of some three dozen drawings by Cartier-Bresson and adding that the artist had especially requested permission to use my fifteen-year-old preface for the catalogue. The dealer wished to learn what fee I would be prepared to receive for publication of this preface. He observed in passing that one of the better drawings to be shown was a portrait of myself. What, I wondered, had become of Henri's doting determination to set aside every single drawing for his daughter? I had no idea. But I was naturally aware that an artist's reputation is served and secured not merely by exhibition but by sale. Creative accomplishment, as Picasso knew better than anyone else, is certified in the marketplace, where Henri had never made an appearance as a draftsman. Besides, if his drawings could be sold for creditable prices, then Melanie's inheritance would profit accordingly. Not that the young woman would ever be pressed for money. Despite his capricious and disaffected ill will, oddly enough, I felt no animosity toward Henri and was perfectly willing that my preface should yet again serve his ambition.

However . . . however, an intriguing, entertaining scheme occurred to me. Never before having thought to be paid for this preface, I thought of it now, since the dealer had put forward the issue.

Moreover, I was curious to know what monetary value Henri put upon works from his hand of a sort never before offered for sale. What, in short, did he feel his fame was worth in cold cash? By asking someone else to ask I learned that the going price would be about twenty-five hundred pounds per drawing, a thumping sum for a beginner but maybe negotiable for a celebrity, which Henri had cunningly become while damning that very condition as degrading and noxious. As it happened, I had recently been paid much more for a catalogue preface, though the exhibition, to be sure, was of works by Alberto. And by 1996 so many portraits of myself had accumulated that I was amused by the prospect of adding one more, especially by a man whose friendship had brusquely been withdrawn. So I wrote to the dealer and told him I did not propose to receive money for permission to publish my text but would be happy to grant it in exchange for my portrait. I did not add that perhaps Henri might interpret my desire to possess this memento as evidence not only of my esteem for his draftsmanship but also as proof that I, at least, harbored no sentiment of ill will. Needless to say, I never found out. Anyway, I got the portrait and hung it behind the door in my dining room underneath a larger and better drawing by Dora.

SZAFRAN

Artists naturally seek out the company of other artists, and those, like myself, who, though not themselves artists, nonetheless seek out their company are inevitably drawn into an exceptional network of camaraderie, common interests, and critical debate. Considering, if one is able, the climactic meaning of art to humankind from birth to death, the companionship of artists is an incomparable source of élan vital. So, in any case, I have found it to be. Thus, in February of 1970, when Raymond Mason introduced me to Sam Szafran, I guessed almost at once that this new and very novel acquaintance might make life not only more interesting but probably much more stimulating. And, indeed, Sam's friendship in time taught me a lot about the relation of artists to their vocation, and the personal price they frequently have to pay for very relative recognition and the passion nevertheless expended without caution. Sometimes Sam reminded me of van Gogh, though his work is by no means comparable and he has known far more professional success during his lifetime. In stature short and thin, but wiry and muscular, with almost an excess of nervous energy, his gaze is unusually piercing and he speaks very rapidly in a rush of compelling self-expression devoted mainly to art, his own art in particular. It is only fair to add that exceptional talent and mercurial versatility provide him with plenty to talk about. The son of Jewish parents who had fled to Paris from Eastern European pogroms, he was six when the Nazis occupied his birthplace, but by dint of cunning stratagems he very narrowly escaped the finality of the Nazi solution, a deliverance not granted to several members of his family. From childhood he had been fascinated with drawing and taught himself by copying cartoons in newspapers and making crude pencil portraits of anyone patient enough to pose. His effective schooling in draftsmanship came entirely from himself, from fifteen years spent in an abandoned garage drawing, drawing, and drawing on any scraps of paper he could find or afford. Paper, pencils, charcoal, and eventually pastels came almost before food as vital necessities. But he did certainly learn to draw with a rapid facility and originality which no École des Beaux-Arts could have taught. It is curious and interesting that painting in oils has never appealed to his talent. Watercolors, yes, but never oils. One wonders why. Oils may not allow for the finesse and *non finito* bravura of his works in other media, especially charcoal.

It was through an exhibition of drawings in charcoal that I first became familiar with Sam's imposing versatility. Many of these were portraits, and I noticed with some surprise and puzzlement that the artist's concentration and technical skill had been devoted to the bodies rather than the facial features of his models. Clearly Sam, unlike his idol, Giacometti, has never been at ease with the human head and its essential gaze. However, it is one of the impressive singularities of his talent as a portraitist that he is often able to convey personal individuality through the expressiveness of the

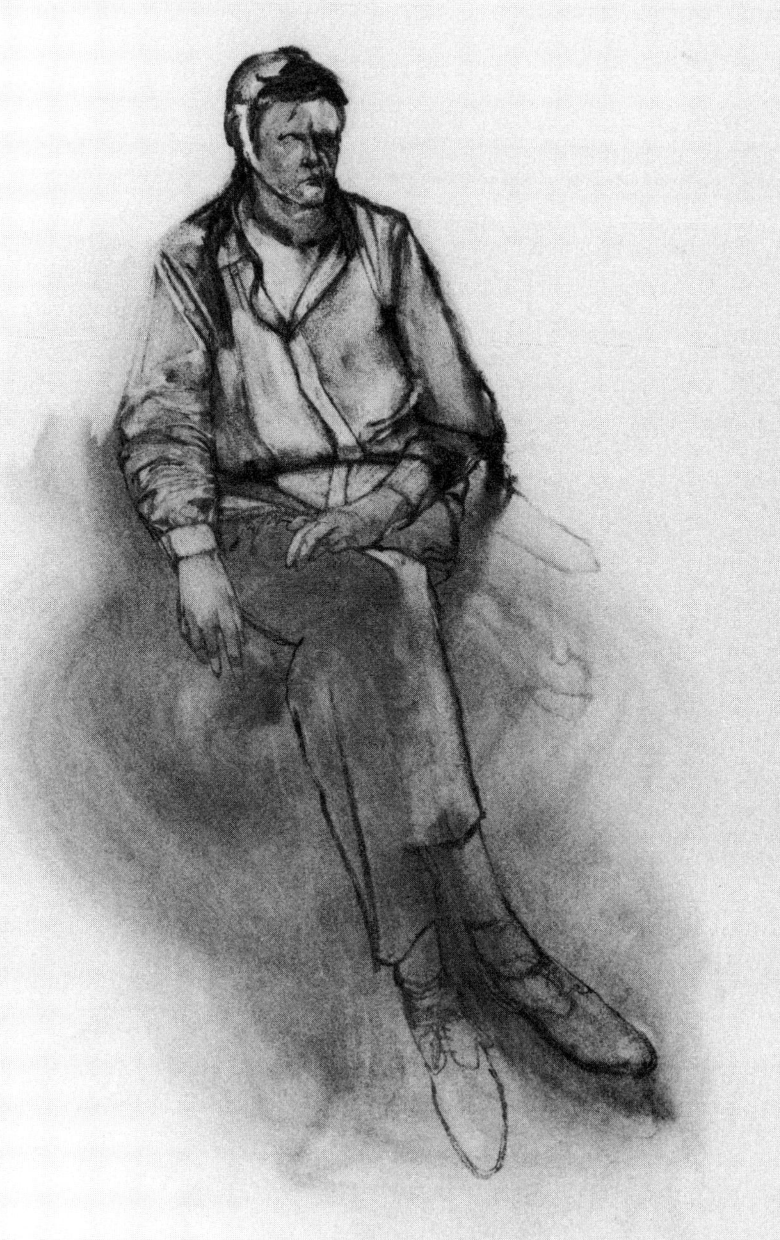

model's unique relation to his own physique. The popular contemporary term "body language" is nonsensical, because articulate vocal sound is limited in connotation to specific words issuing from the mouth alone. But hands and feet, arms, legs, torsos and heads, viewed with perspicacity and situated with visionary intuition in relation to each other can express almost—almost!—as much about an individual's nature as the configuration and appearance of his countenance. It was in this unusual aspect of portraiture that Sam excelled.

His favored and obsessive subjects for representation, however, were not people but views of his studio overgrown with tropical plants, his wife—a live presence in this jungle—and also a seemingly interminable series of imaginary staircases perceived from contortionist points of view. In 1972 I composed a long article for *L'Oeil* about Sam's studio and staircase pastels, then much later—in 1987—my preface introduced the catalogue for an exhibition in New York of truly remarkable watercolors of very similar subjects. All artists are unpredictable and esoteric, therefore exceptionally difficult to write about, and Sam—knowingly?—has always been more esoteric and unpredictable than most. To attempt to write about him has, therefore, from the first been an exhilarating but daunting challenge. Today I am consequently relieved to try only to look with a little clairvoyance at a couple of the dozen or so portraits that he drew of me in half an afternoon sometime in 1973.

It came from him as an unexpected whim that he asked me to pose, but Sam was nothing if not whimsical, and I was, as usual, willing. He sat quite close to me in his studio, no more than four or five feet away, with large sheets of paper propped on a portfolio, and yet the drawings he made appear to set the model at a mental distance. The first, the only one inscribed to me, is the most typical of his forte for conveying an individual's inner characteristics via the sensitively rendered and stylistically original representation of a body mostly concealed by clothes. Little is left to the haphazard dictation of mere appearances. The position of hands, arms, legs, and feet composes in itself a revelation of the model's individuality even as it expresses the artist's bravura technique. The relations of tonality and form are deliberately chosen and stated in expressive terms, conveying by the indications of mass and elements of design a fine, scrupulous artistic sense. The placement of the head is anatomically precise but the treatment of the face—suggestive of intemperate belligerence—is in bizarre contrast to the placid composure of the bodily portrait. This may be an intimation of the contradictory aggressiveness which sometimes characterized Sam's personal behavior. The drawing, in any case, executed with confident dash and rapidity, is a powerful and evocative work of art.

Unlike the first, the second portrait I have selected to reproduce is impressive as an example of the artist's versatility at the expense, so to speak, of the model. Only a hint this time of facial likeness suggests the personal identity of the seated figure. And yet this hint imbues the entire hastily and arbitrarily rendered image with a haunting individuality. It is the perverse secret of Sam's remarkable talent to be able to conjure from a glimpse a stirring metaphysical presence situated in deliberate and enduring space. To be able to do so much with so little so rapidly is invaluable as a contribution to high art in a time when reassurance as to its viable future has become invaluable.

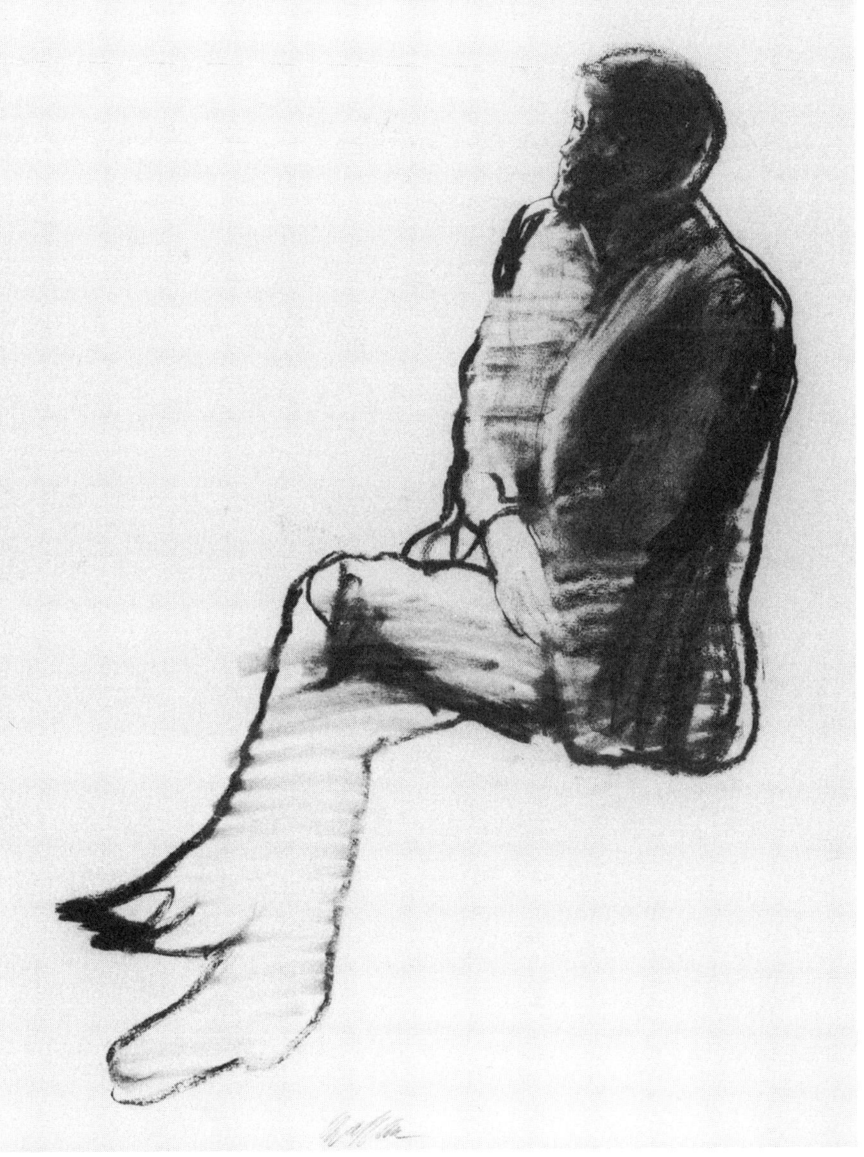

TOUBEAU

Yet again the acquaintance of one artist led to acquaintance with another, and it was once more through the companionable good will of Raymond Mason that early in March of 1975 I met a young painter aged only twenty-nine named Jean-Max Toubeau. He invited me to visit his studio. The paintings and drawings I saw there were inventive and accomplished, I felt, the work of a determined artist who had known how to put to refined and subtle effect the traditional training he'd received. The subject matter was varied: numerous complex still lifes, interiors, figure studies, and landscapes, these last obviously views of Provence. His family, I learned, owned a house in Gordes, a picturesque town just across the valley from Ménerbes. It may have been a shared attachment to this enchanting landscape that brought about the friendship between Raymond and his young colleague. Jean-Max had also executed a series of portraits of a well-known French author, a distant cousin, and had a propensity for portraiture. He later became a close friend of Cartier-Bresson, whom he sought to assist (with little resourcefulness) in the complexities of draftsmanship. His knowledge of art history and of the technical properties of painting is extensive and serious. He is an excellent talker, able to elucidate with imposing specificity the means by which artists as diverse as Vermeer, Velázquez, Rembrandt, or Cézanne achieved comparable aesthetic effects by very unlike means. It is an irony and a paradox of the painterly vocation, however, that sometimes those able to express themselves almost more effectively in spoken terms than in visual ones dissipate the very power of expression which they most firmly aspire to cultivate. There were, indeed, moments in conversation with Jean-Max when I felt that I had been transformed into the one-man audience of a lecture. But it is not apposite here to analyze the evolution of his personal or professional development as a painter or, for that matter, as an individual.

A few months after our first encounter, during which period we enjoyed numerous friendly meetings in his studio or my apartment or in cafés and restaurants, Jean-Max came to visit me at home, where I was recovering from the flu. It was a yellow afternoon in May—the twenty-ninth, to be precise. He had with him a sketchbook and asked whether I would pose for a drawing, an invitation which I think I've never refused. It took some time, this drawing, an hour or more, longer than most of the former portraits, for Jean-Max was as studious in work as in conversation. Insofar as it was a replica of what I thought to see when looking in the mirror, I felt satisfied by the outcome. The image that looked at me looked like me, I felt, but it remained a mirror image, removed by artifice from the actual subject no matter how closely one looked. Just as the mirror image stays always at a remove behind the glass surface, so Jean-Max's drawing seems to remain beyond the surface of the page, appealing but elusive, a portrait of a phantom person closely resem-

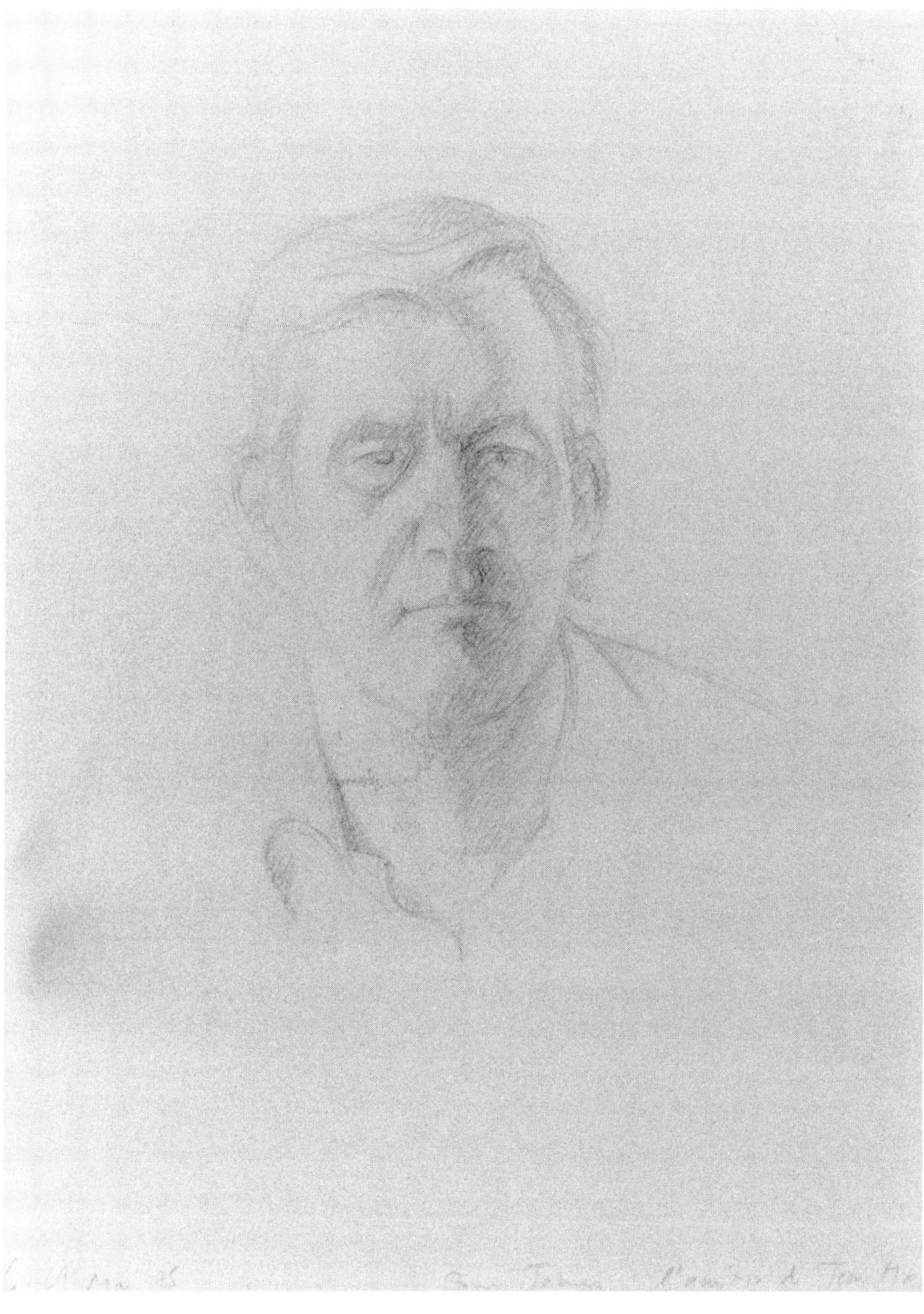

bling James Lord. The eyes are carefully drawn, and yet their life-affirming gaze is absent. And so it is with the rest: competent as a likeness but inert as a portrait. The drawing is pleasing, too pleasing perhaps, for in the passion to please the visionary vitality of the creative force majeure oftentimes fades. Still, Jean-Max's careful drawing does provide pleasurable company, and I am glad of its friendly capacity to do that.

We continued friends for some years. I later visited him at his parents' home in Gordes. In 1980 an exhibition of his paintings and drawings was arranged in Paris and I wrote a preface for the catalogue. As Jean-Max became more and more friendly with Cartier-Bresson, however, while I became less and less so, we gradually ceased to meet very often, finally not at all save for chance encounters at exhibitions. When, as I've said, I look with pleasure at Jean-Max's portrait, I enjoy a happy sense of the vital good that flows from an awareness of life's brevity and art's longevity.

THEIMER

Alberto used to say that the best place to meet people was in the street, because it was there that the greatest variety and greatest number were to be found. I've met quite a few, and with pleasurable consequences, but only one happened to be an artist and became a lasting friend. Our meeting, as it happens, was not entirely accidental, because the stranger was accompanied by an acquaintance, an art dealer interested in his work who introduced us briefly on the sidewalk. As I live in a neighborhood densely provided with art galleries, it was no surprise to occasionally encounter again this stocky, dark-haired, foreign-looking fellow. We would say hello, nothing more. I did not think, or care, that he might be an artist. This was in the spring of 1985.

My friend Gilles and I had recently fallen into the habit of spending our summers in rented villas on the luxuriant hillsides surrounding the Tuscan town of Lucca, which I had first visited a quarter of a century before with Harold Acton. In this magical place (uncontaminated by tourists) we easily made friends. A couple of the closest owned an antique shop which now and then doubled as an art gallery. So what was my surprise—a pleasant one—to find that they were friends of the Parisian stranger, who also lived nearby, an artist, moreover, a sculptor, but also skilled in painting. His name: Ivan Theimer. Aged just forty, as I learned later, he was indeed by birth foreign, Czech, from an industrial city a couple of hundred kilometers east of Prague, not a promising locality for the encouragement of creative aspirations. He had managed, however, to gain admission to an art school in a nearby town, where exceptional talent was recognized, and at the rash age of twenty-three had fled from his Communist homeland to impoverished freedom in Paris. Being skilled and resourceful, a few industrious years sufficed to make a paying place for him in the city which had nurtured the fulfillment of so many artists from abroad.

Theimer went out of his way to be friendly, and he excelled at it. He took us to choice but out-of-the-way restaurants and introduced us to a number of interesting people, including a delightful patroness of the arts who owned an immense villa built on a hilltop by Napoleon for his sister Elisa. She also owned a number of works by Theimer. They roused my curiosity, and the artist proved cordially prepared to satisfy it. He took me to his studio across the mountains in the town of Pietrasanta, where in a cavernous, dingy, acrid foundry his works were cast in bronze. So in one day I must have seen fifty of his creations, and I was surprised. In the context of art being produced at that time, or even today, for that matter, there was decidedly nothing that began for one minute to resemble the sculpture of Theimer. What it did resemble—and resemble, one might say, with an audacious vengeance—was the sculpture of the Hellenistic era and of Imperial Rome. There were many obelisks, bas-reliefs with draped figures, portrait busts on elegant pedestals,

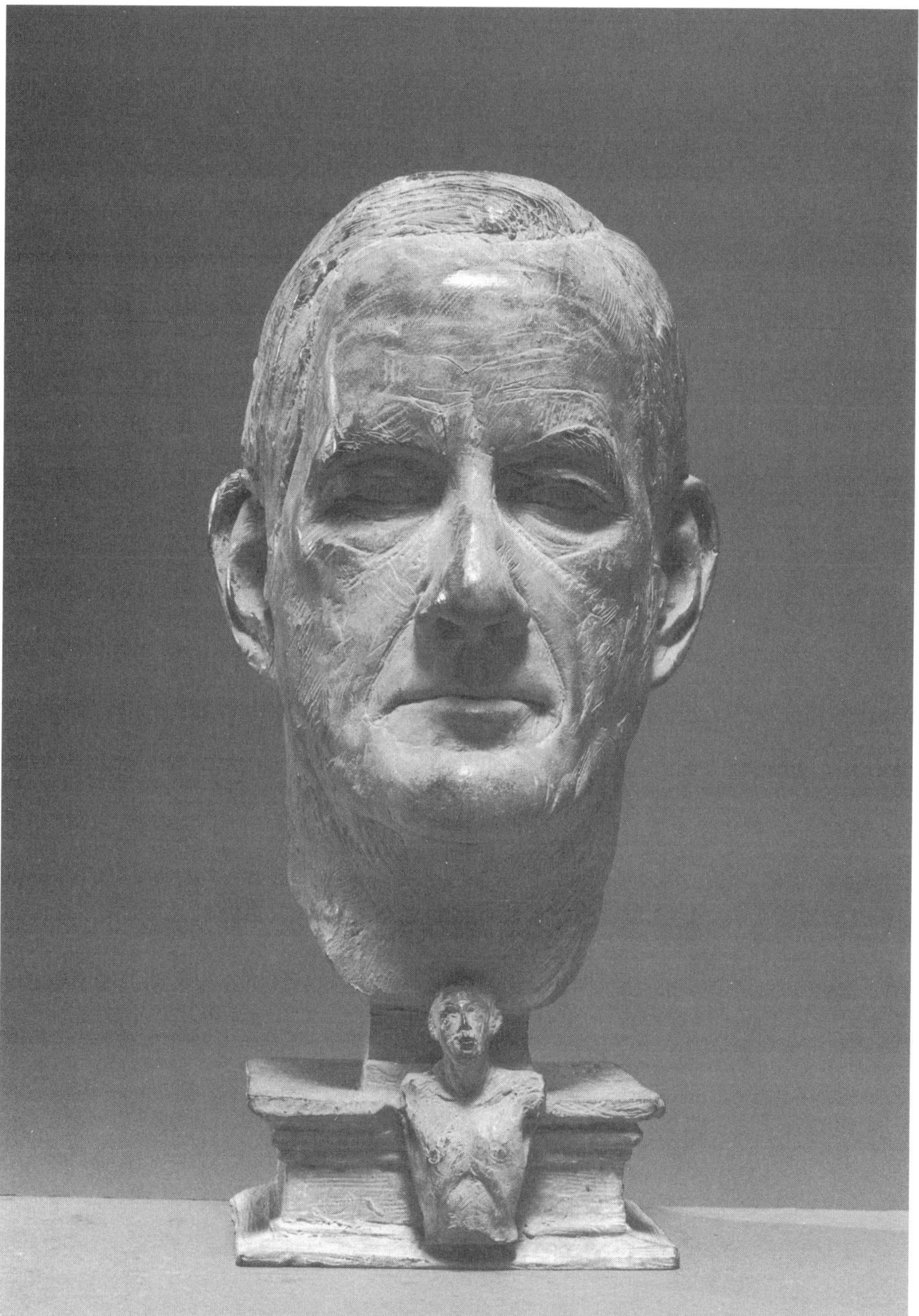

tortoises, serpents, seashells, porcupines, and a great variety of decorative medallions. The overt resemblance, however, dexterously avoided the easy pitfall of pastiche, for this artist obviously saw that the adventure which interests posterity does not take that path. Theimer has clearly found in the art of classical antiquity, with an occasional, invigorating hint of pagan mysticism, the rich store of symbols and forms suited to the expressive needs of his temperament. The great men of the well-named Renaissance sought, and discovered, greatness by adding to the mystic immanence of the antique sensibility a well-wrought measure of humanist warmth and responsiveness to the wealth of nature. The sole, entire purpose of artistic creation is the completion of works of art, not the satisfaction of the artist. This is a metaphysical rule. Theimer, I felt, created convincing evidence of his obedience to it, providing for others, incidentally, welcome access to the mysterious sources of aesthetic gratification. He spoke with unassuming eloquence of the works that he showed me, making no issue of their patent technical prowess or stylistic ingenuity. I responded with honest and pensive admiration. It was easy, after all, to affirm that I had seen no other work comparable to his own in imaginative originality. When he asked whether my appreciation might yield some written commentary, I said, "Why not?" Being on vacation, I had nothing but my journal in hand. To write about Theimer's sculpture, having unpredictably come upon it there in Lucca, could qualify as material for the journal, anyway. I knew very well that I couldn't value it as comparable in any way to Alberto's works, but I was intrigued by this transient assignment.

So I sat down for an hour or so every afternoon and waited, as always, with happy anxiety for words with some shimmer of reasoned meaning to materialize from nothingness. And after four or five days something like a text did materialize, though whether it actually shimmered with any illumination of reason I wouldn't presume to suppose. Anyway, there was a lavish bouquet of rhetoric that could intelligibly be translated into praise and the artist was pleased.

In Paris, Ivan had a studio in the long row of pre-1914 studios facing the gardens of the Observatory. At his suggestion I visited him there occasionally. We would have lunch afterward in a nearby brasserie, talk about Donatello or Dubuffet or the Soviet repression of the homeland. We became friends. It was in mid-January of 1986 when he proposed to model a portrait bust of me. I posed for a couple of hours every afternoon for six consecutive days in the first week of February, seated only a few feet from the sculptor. I had often seen Alberto at work on his sculptures of heads or figures and didn't expect Ivan to proceed in a manner at all similar. Alberto, after all, was working toward a conceptual absolute by definition unattainable, whereas Ivan's creative aim was the production of a pleasing, sometimes surprising, stylistically imposing work of art. He did not insist on complete immobility, so I was able to observe the extraordinary dexterity with which a sizable lump of clay evolved little by little from formless mud into a gradual semblance of humanity, as if the gradual evolution of the species from primordial slime unto Darwin himself were taking place at the speed of light. While he worked, Ivan several times exclaimed, "My God, how I'm flattering you. I'm flattering you to death." Maybe he meant to evoke the likely survival of the bronze for far longer than that of flesh. Or perhaps it was the cultural, anthropological, metaphysical superiority of art in comparison to the trivial nonsense of human struggle that stirred him. Or he may merely have been moved by his facility for flattery. As to that, wrinkles here and there may have been subjected to tact. But I think the bust by and large is only too sharp as a likeness, and that may be the severest criticism I could make of it. The recall of antiquity is resonant, though I don't resemble a Roman senator or Renaissance humanist. There is no clear precedent for Theimer's work, and it exists peculiarly in the present as if outside of time, as if Houdon, Canova, and Rodin, not to mention Epstein, Picasso, and Giacometti, had never existed. In an odd way this is a source of power, because there is no gainsaying the forceful presence of his figures and faces.

My bust is to me a detached but tangible representation of a remote, austere, unsmiling individual whom I nevertheless recognize as the model to whom this bronze object is insensibly indebted. The metallic gaze is cast coldly downward, inscrutable, the lips compressed, emotionless, the thrust of the chin severe. Whatever else I may seem to do or to be, I don't believe I speak to myself in the language of that face.

Below the formal pedestal Ivan added a tiny, impish man staring fixedly forward, his mouth agape, as if he were calling out hopelessly to the infinity of art in the demented expectation that from it some pitiable redemption might be forthcoming.

A RUSSIAN ARTIST

In all the world there are at best but half a dozen great capital cities to vie with each other as supremely beautiful. After Paris, I think, St. Petersburg comes second. There's Rome, to be sure, but it's rather a hodgepodge of splendor, ruin, the merely picturesque, and Mussolini monstrosity. Venice, of course, is hors concours, and a small place by today's criteria. Anyway, in the late springtime of 1995, Gilles and I spent ten thrilling days in St. Petersburg and its glorious environs.

After dinner on Sunday, May 25th, we came out of our hotel and strolled up the Nevsky Prospect. It was then still light, the famous White Nights having already commenced, and the sinking sun sent a roseate gleam across the colonnaded façade of the Mikhailovsky Palace on the other side of the avenue. To our right lay a small park, its pathways lined by lofty trees. We didn't know it then but soon found out that this was called the Square of the Arts, because a theater, concert hall, and museum occupy three sides of it, while the statue of a man reading from a book stands in the center. Naturally, this was none other than Pushkin, as we were somewhat sniffily informed. No sooner had we wandered into this park than we were accosted by several men volunteering to draw our portraits. And what, indeed, could have been more logical than a gathering of artists in the Square of the Arts? Six or seven of them pressed forward to display samples of their handiwork, and to our surprise it looked impressive, not at all the sort of crude caricature trash commonplace in Paris, Venice, or St. Tropez. These men were artists who had obviously received rigorous traditional training in stylistic representation. All of them were aged fifty or more and I thought that perhaps now that the strictures of Socialist realism were finished, maybe they felt finished, too, left behind by youths infatuated with chic works made in the U.S.A. by the likes of Rauschenberg, Twombly, Schnabel, et al. And, indeed, competition with such company would have been direly disheartening for anyone taught to admire, and emulate, conventional idols such as Ilya Repin. It was, consequently, with some sense of compassion that I consented to have one of these artists draw my portrait.

I chose a man probably aged over sixty, gaunt and poorly dressed, whose sample portraits were small, barely larger than a postcard, sketched in pencil with evident rapidity but vigorous skill, and suggested a flair for catching a likeness. He spoke a smattering of English. I was asked to stand still while he kept slightly to one side but only a few feet away and studied my face intently for several minutes. Then he began to draw rapidly on his small sheet of paper, glancing toward me only two or three times, for the finished drawing was done in less than five minutes. When I saw it, I felt at once that instinct had led me to an artist of authentic talent, though, to be sure, a talent molded by the aesthetic criteria of a bygone era. This somewhat anachronistic aspect, however, does not diminish the drawing's effectiveness as a portrait any more than would be true of

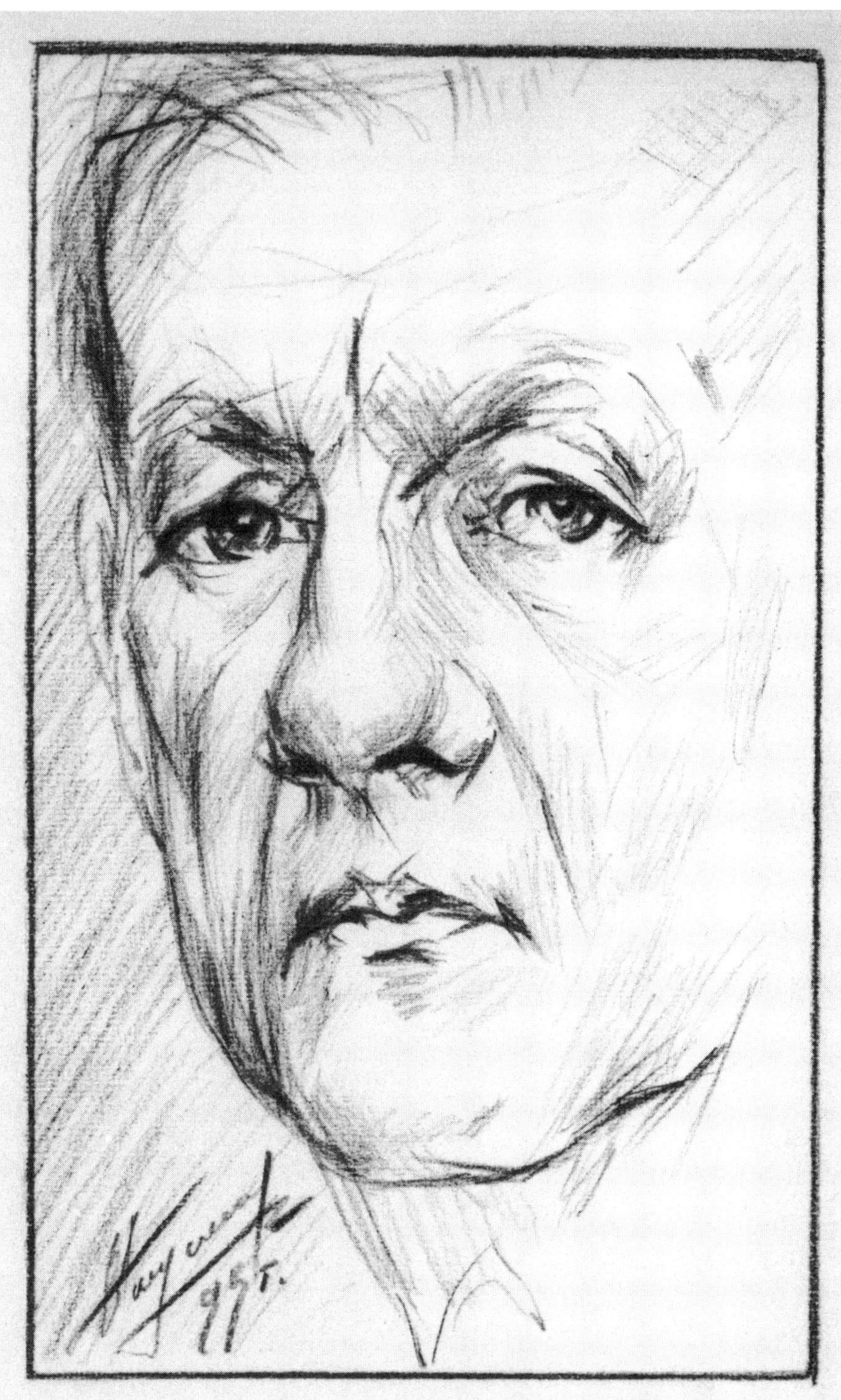

a sketch by Sargent, whose informal portrait drawings are not very dissimilar or much more accomplished, in fact, than the work executed by this Russian artist more than a century later. Indeed, the Russian portrait is quite as competent in capturing a model's likeness and vitality as many of Sargent's painted portraits, particularly those unflawed by a bent for flattery. The striking power of this small drawing is initially expressed in the formal representation of a head bearing the structure of personal features emphatically my own: the stark emotional intensity of the eyes, stern stamp of the mouth, and cast of the chin. The immediacy of the portrait derives largely from the rapid virtuosity with which it was executed. It is one of the liveliest likenesses of the many that have been made, though by no means among the finest renderings artistically. And yet it possesses a compelling authority all its own, resembling no other. Perhaps this singularly distinctive character is one consequence of its creation by an artist forged from a culture foreign to the occidental formation of the other artists represented here. In the depths of his responsive but unconscious eye certainly dwelt influential reminiscences of ancient icons imbued by the traditions of Byzantium.

When it was finished, signed, dated, and handed to me, I expressed my appreciation as feelingly as I could. The artist, I thought, took enthusiasm rather for granted. The price was almost absurdly low. I urged Gilles to pose as well, which he did and with no less satisfaction than mine. Who the artist was I would have liked to know, but his signature is indecipherable not only for me but also for the Russian friends to whom I've shown the drawing. And maybe this is strangely appropriate, because the haunting portraits of Republican Rome are all anonymous, and there is an eerie similarity between them and the drawing of the anonymous Russian.

SÉCHERET

The Parisian street where I live, named the rue des Beaux-Arts because the school stands at its west end, is a short one, accommodating but seventeen perfectly commonplace apartment buildings. The places of business at street level, however—save one ostentatious hotel, a student café, and a shop selling artists' materials—are noteworthy because all of them are in the very same commercial pursuit, dealing in a commodity called art. Twenty-seven galleries are located on this single thoroughfare, of which the name must seem predestined to dealers. Only a few pretend to much distinction, and even they mostly cater to the trade in fashionable junk or objects of dubious provenance and debatable aesthetic intent conveniently characterized as "tribal."

Six decades of gazing into gallery windows have made me content to be blasé. It is very seldom now that I glimpse anything I like, rare indeed that I see something to admire, and nearly never that I'm stricken by the acquisitive fever, long ago so powerfully exciting. And so it was absolutely astonishing one afternoon in November 1983, while strolling along the south side of my street, to behold a painting in a gallery window that stopped me still where I stood. I naturally knew the gallery. It was an offshoot of the École des Beaux-Arts, reserved for exhibitions of work by students deemed particularly gifted, and for years I had observed with ennui countless impotent, misbegotten duplications of international inanity. But here all at once in this supremely unpromising locale was a picture that looked like an authentic work of art. Going inside, I found approximately a score of others, several of them as fine, or almost, as the one which had first surprised me. All were landscapes, painted with a representational flair that would have impressed Sisley or Pissarro. A young man with wiry blond hair and Nordic eyes was alone in the gallery. I inquired. He was the artist, of course, shy but self-confident, named Jean-Baptiste Sécheret. He gave me a mimeographed checklist of the works on exhibit. Yes, he said, they were for sale. The painting I had seen from the sidewalk was the one I judged not only finest but most appealing, a view of mountaintops, hillsides, valleys, and forests, in which a lonely stretch of road was the only sign of human presence. It could have been an early Corot reworked by Daubigny reworked by Sécheret, and there was no mistaking a nostalgia for the nineteenth century. I shared it, having never appreciated abstract painting, expressionist or otherwise, though a splash of decorative color demanding no mental or spiritual faculty can be superficially attractive. The picture I admired was not expensive. When I asked the artist to reserve it for me and told him my name, it came out that he had heard of me, having read some of my writing about Giacometti. I visited the exhibition several times. We became friendly. I still admire with careful scrutiny the painting I acquired that first day, though now I own at least a dozen others, illustrative of a rational maturity.

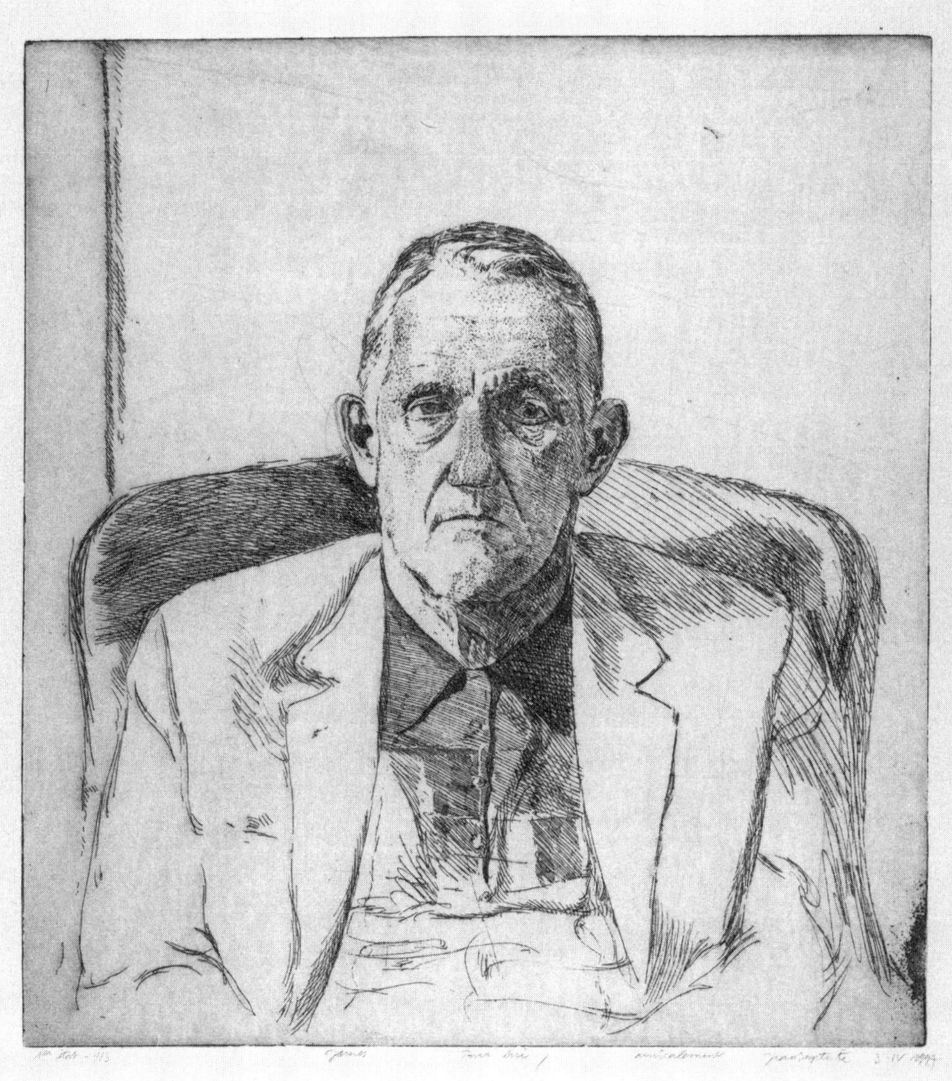

In the image he creates the artist dwells. In his art resides the power and subtlety with which he develops the resources of a viewer's imagination. Technical power signifies that the imaginary wherewithal of an image represents an artist's will to identify his solitary perception with a potentially universal view. And it was in the modality of such ideas—or ideals—that young Sécheret developed the imagery of his art. He never entirely set aside representation, but nineteenth-century nostalgia subsided in an evolution toward mature skill and stylistic virtuosity. An ingenious variety of subject matter was synthesized with resourceful technical self-discipline. He worked with equal dexterity and to high effect in oils, watercolor, pen and ink, pencil, copperplate etching, monotype, and lithograph. Rare, indeed, are artists whose gift flows with such capable spontaneity from one ticklish technique to another. The subject matter is appropriately arresting, too: still lifes of all sorts of objects, especially funnels, for a time, then landscapes, seascapes, interiors, buildings, portraits, as if he were testing his hand in the difficulty of antithetical diversity. Sécheret is an arbitrary nonconformist, consequently the master of his ambition and not on easy terms with art dealers, to most of whom the artist's work is appraised in terms of sales. Still, he has enjoyed considerable professional success.

As I say, we became friendly. I liked the company of his wife and children. And when after some years he proposed to paint my portrait, the prospect seemed as natural as daylight. It was not a success. I posed every afternoon for a week, but the only element of the portrait satisfactory to the painter turned out to be my necktie. The canvas got painted over and we forgot about it. Then in 1989 he made a small portrait etching, which as an etching was skilled, as a portrait, however, dourly unlike the model. Since we continued to meet frequently, there were other attempts, none of them acceptable to the artist, hence destroyed. He was conscientious and persistent, though.

Late in March of 1997 he asked me to pose yet again, this time for a large etching, reproduced here as No. 1. It required several patient, immobile sittings, but the result proved satisfying to both Sécheret and myself. As an etching it clearly is the outcome of prolonged and steadfast concentration on technical finesse in a traditional style. As an image it is a powerful depiction of the visual rapport between artist and model, each purposefully intent upon a work of art independent of both. As a likeness it possesses a stern resemblance to the model, vigilant and austere, but more than this it gazes forth from the page with the authority of vital permanence which resides only in works of art. Thus it is akin to the mortal purpose and metaphysical perpetuation of the extraordinary portraits from Faiyum. Not easy to live with, perhaps, it is quite impossible at the same time to disregard.

As content with his etching as ever an artist can honestly be, Jean-Baptiste determined to have me pose for a monotype. This is a very different technical product, the subject being painted with ink directly onto a copper plate and printed immediately, providing but a single image. Several of these were made, the one reproduced here being the last and the only print to satisfy the artist. It is obviously very different from the etching. The immediacy of technique and of perception are evident. Between artist and model there is no strain now to endow a portrait with vital intensity. It is quick, easy, lyrical; the model's gaze and the artist's expressive skill indicate the famil-

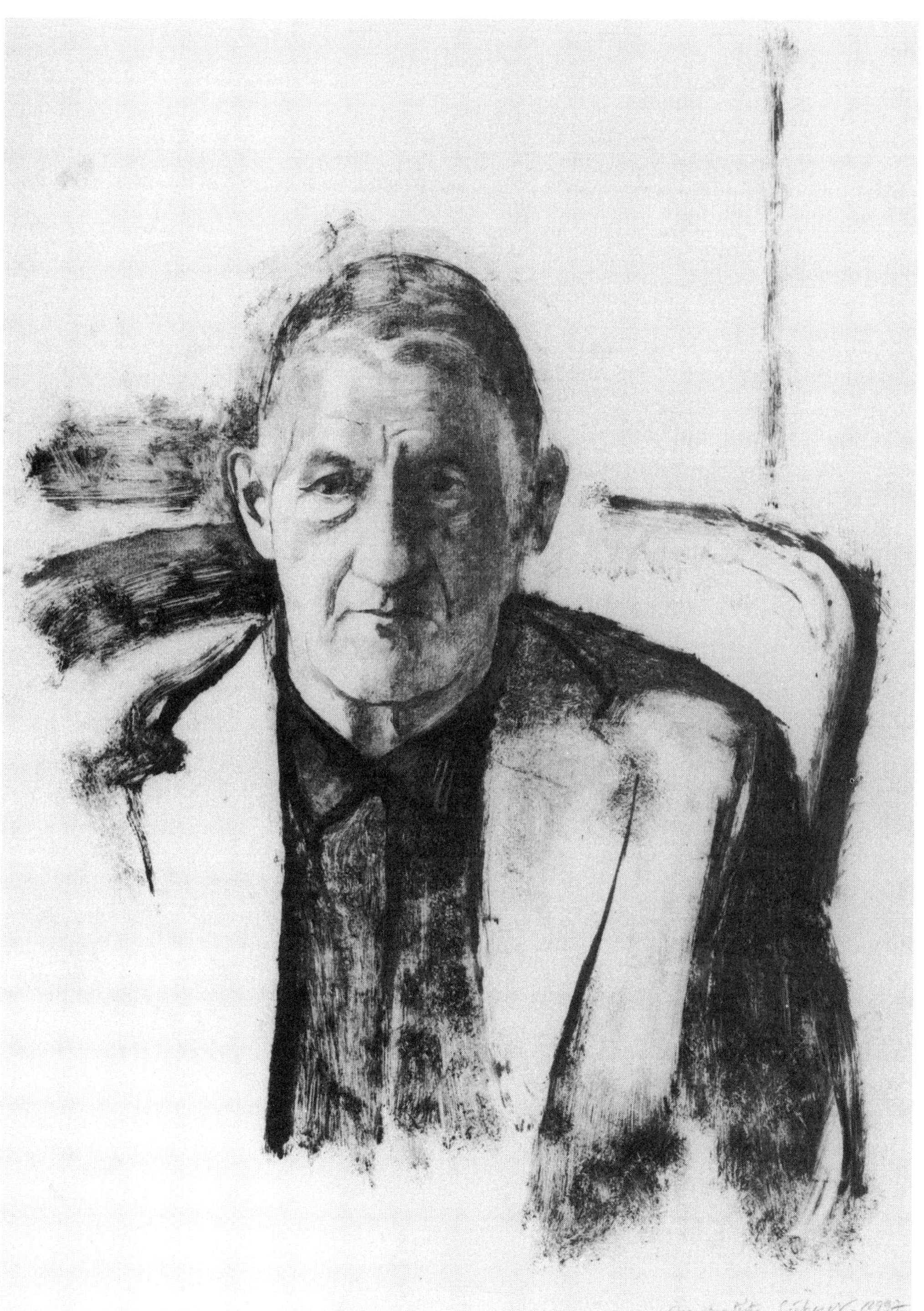
James

iarity of friendship, not the grave adumbration of a metaphysical purpose. If the model's half-smile is quizzical, the artist's sensitive representation is the response of creative pleasure. Of the two portraits, therefore, the less accomplished is the more likable. When awakening each morning, I see this image of a believable self as my first glimpse of a speculative world, and that is a pleasing intimation of reality.

CORDELL

Of the numerous portraits of me, few make use of color, and only two of those reproduced in this volume exploit chromatic variety to convey character. The watercolor by Mason is one, the oil painting by Cordell the other. It is, indeed, a revelation of the singular talents of the two artists that the use of color by each is as telling and vital to their representational purposes as competent draftsmanship could be in another hand. To show these two paintings in black and white is consequently to incur some loss of nuance—a loss very different in each instance—and yet the essential definition of both portraits is kept faithfully present.

Only four American artists have had the rash and generous diligence to make my portrait, and of these four the most American in creative temperament and native feeling is Thomas Cordell. Thus, he is a fundamentally traditional artist. His paintings reflect with lyrical originality the characteristic that has been most fruitful for American art since the early nineteenth century: direct inspiration by nature. It was the majesty, the purity, the fertility, and the diversity of the American landscape—rather than the exotic aspect of its inhabitants—that most provided subject matter for our finest painters until in 1913 the Armory Show and later the First World

War radically altered—for better or for worse—the pure and innocent vision intrinsic to our land.

By tenacious spirit and hard work Cordell has made of himself and his art the legitimate offspring of our traditional "old masters," men seldom equaled in our young culture: Winslow Homer, George Inness, Ralph Blakelock, Childe Hassam, Edward Hopper, and Fairfield Porter, to name only the most accomplished. Talent and character are not the same thing, and the former without the latter is likely to turn out tinsel. It glitters, to be sure, but life expectancy is fated to be brief. Possessing both character and talent, Cordell's paintings are unequivocally—one might almost say defiantly—figurative, make no moral, political, or pseudo-aesthetic statements, and scrupulously avoid the temptation to be fashionable. They simply challenge the viewer to open his mind as well as his eyes. What one perceives is that this artist has disciplined his vision to harmonize with his hand in order to draw well. Giacometti repeatedly said that drawing is the basic component of all valid art. But skill as a draftsman is far from all that's required to make a competent, convincing, complete painter. He must attain such intimacy with the potential of his materials that composition, color, brush stroke all become not only the outgrowth of his subject matter but also a vital aspect of his well-being. He must so discipline his spiritual identification with what he does that it becomes a fully realized expression of who he is. Such self-revelation demands the audacity of true humility, but there is no other way to mastery. And I have known Tom well enough and long enough—call it a quarter of a century—to believe that he has progressed appreciably well along that road so rarely traveled on.

I call the artist Tom because he is my friend, as most of those have been who bothered to do my portrait. Of them all, certainly, he

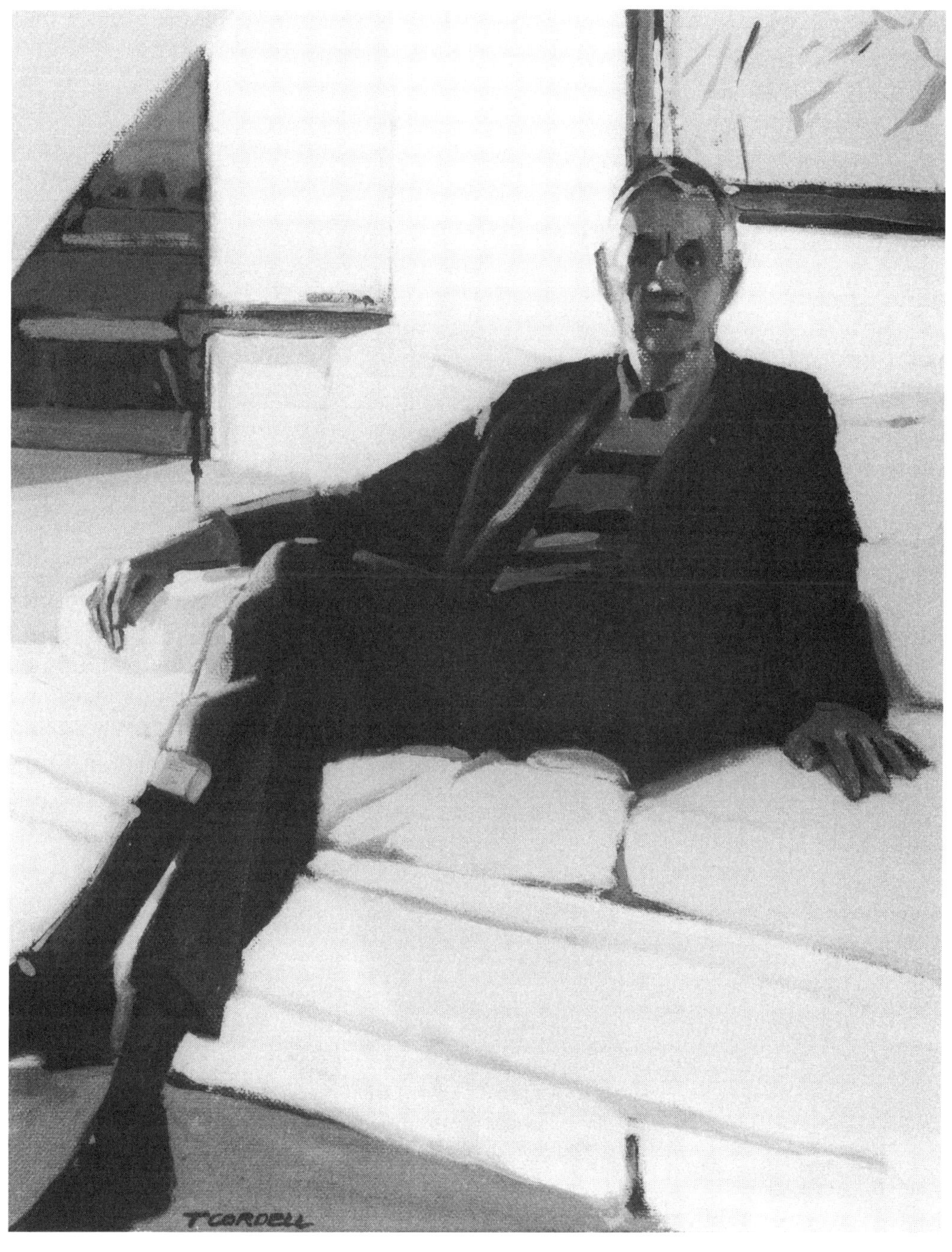
T CORDELL

has been one of the friendliest, and his portrait speaks with feeling of our compatibility. It does not strive to make an imposing metaphysical statement but succeeds with uncanny finesse, almost, that is, without technical effort, in representing my personality as well as my person, and that is doubtless in large part because in this image my entire body is shown in an intimate environment and in its bearing expresses a more expansive and evocative likeness than the face alone. There is no other portrait of me that resembles this one, and yet it resembles me with a deft fidelity that issues from the evident ease of its execution. It also resembles Tom in its truth to a highly disciplined vision that takes no particular for granted but dwells upon detail with the simple virtuosity of charm. Charm, indeed, it possesses in abundance more than is mine—but that is its friendliness—and brings to the mind's eye some of Homer's early pictures of children playing. One need only note the highlights on the knuckles of the right hand, the tip of the nose, the trousers of the left leg. And the model's yielding gaze, like his posture, is demonstrative of congenial relinquishment to the prerogative of the artist. A black-and-white photograph cannot convey the subtle gradation in the color between the right end of the couch and the left, a transition from bright cream to the palest blue-violet, such a delicate nuance as one might look for in Manet.

But this is a very American work of art. In his creativity, as I've remarked, Cordell is more American than most of his compatriot painters. Though I am depicted in the salon of my Parisian apartment, and by turning my head I could see the façade of the Louvre, I am American, the artist is American, and the painting is American, and if ever I succumbed to the haunting affliction of homesickness, Tom's portrait would provide beautiful first aid.

LENNARD

Despite my belief that images made by machines cannot be classified as works of art in the same sphere of cultural distinction as those made by human hands it seems admissible to contend that a machine-made image subsequently made over to some extent by hand may partake of a specialized aesthetic character determined by the duality, so to speak, of this creation. That is why I have chosen to include amongst these portraits the quartered photographic image retouched in gouache by Elizabeth Lennard, my fourth compatriot artist, and like myself a long-time resident of Paris.

Lizzie has been professionally occupied with machine-made images for twenty-five years, and not only those which are static but also many which move. To her credit she has made about a dozen lively, interesting, and original films which have been shown to critical acclaim in Paris, New York, and many European cities, including Moscow. She has even published several volumes of her reworked, painted photographs illustrating texts by Gertrude Stein. If I mention the variety of her professional undertakings, it is to emphasize the seriousness of her creative commitment as well as the successful versatility she has wrought from it.

It was in early August of 1997 that Lizzie came to visit at the country house where I then spent the summertime in the southeast corner of France; and there on the terrace in front of the house in the late afternoon she made the photographs—many more than four—which here appear as a quadruple yet single portrait. It is no simple matter for the model of a photograph—let alone four of them simultaneously—to appraise the apparent self paralyzed as an image on a piece of paper. There is no rapport with a subjective resemblance executed by an impersonal hand guided by an objective eye, however friendly. As a likeness a photograph lacks life. Even in the image of a child there is a prefiguration of death, because the machine stops time, whereas a painting or drawing conveys the ecstatic intimation of immortality, for its human creation places it—independent of aesthetic value—in the timeless context of history alongside the portraits of Jan Six and Victor Chocquet. Not that I mean to belittle Ms. Lennard's work or artistic integrity. Her creativity is authentic and honorable. What I hoped to write about was the resemblance between Lizzie's photographs, whether painted or not, and the image I see—if I can tolerate to stare at it—when I look in the mirror. As I have noted, Jean Cocteau often said that gazing into the mirror was to come face-to-face with the image of death. Allowing for poetic license, in which there is ample latitude for truth, a trillionth of a second of cosmological time verifies the accuracy of the poet's "bon" mot. And when I study Lizzie's photos, I seem to see them on the far side of the glass, thus as illusions, extensions of reflected light rays that merely appear to intersect behind the actual surface, as if I were able to perceive in an altered dimension of experience and time the presence of a being I can only

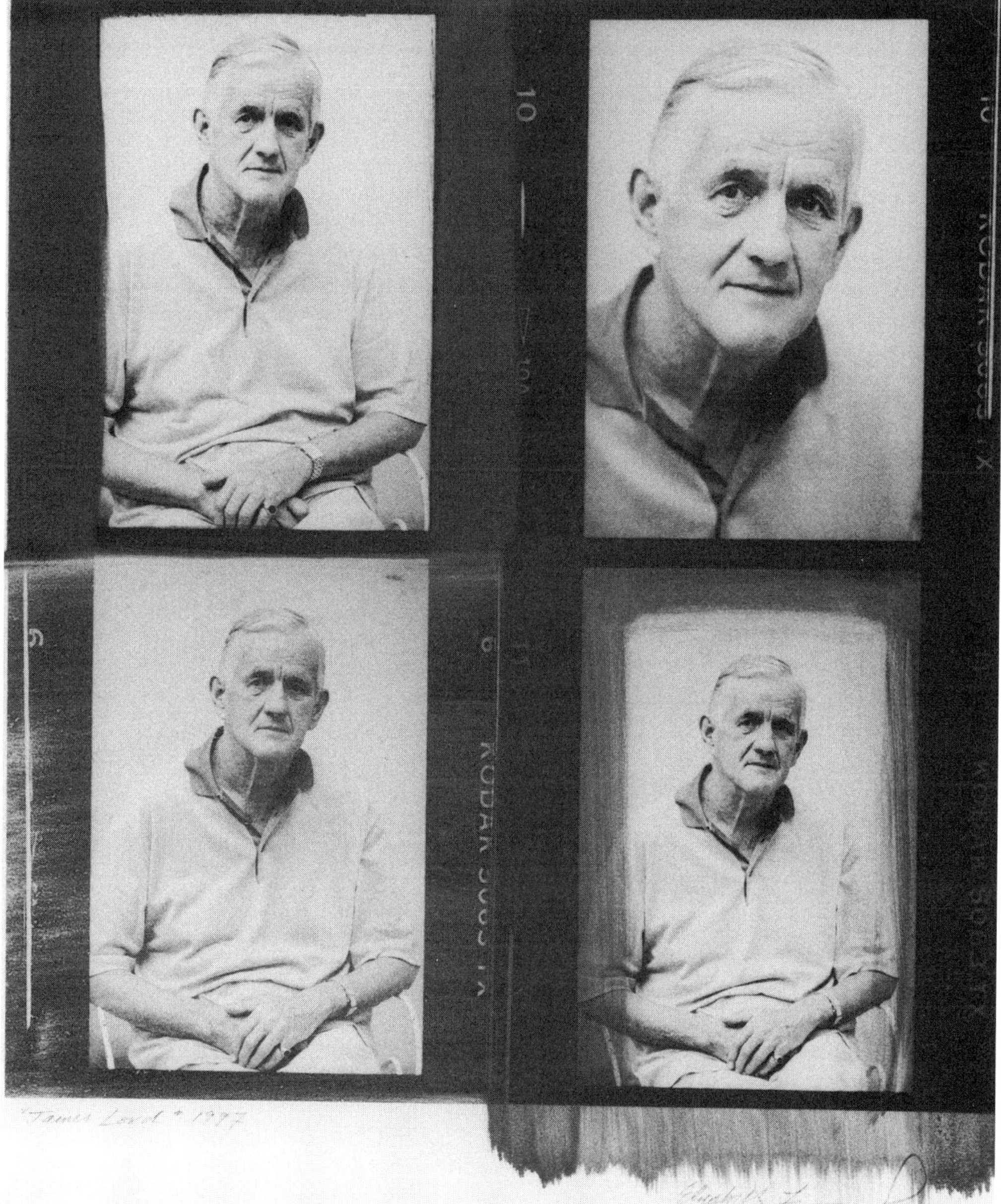
"James Lord" 1997

conjecture to recognize as myself: looking backward, as it were, through the vista of light so frequently evoked by those whose life functions have temporarily, seemingly, ceased, only to resume in extremis thanks to therapeutic intervention.

These photographs, then, become memento mori of a sort. If I have—and I have—some life in the drawn and painted portraits, survival is a supposition fraught with uncertainty in the camera images of someone soon to die. Only my wristwatch and ring seem assured of enduring reality, and they already appear to adorn a ghost. In this, to be sure, there is an aesthetic element. Something decisive has been expressed about the human situation with dynamic and vital effect. This is not a transcendent act of origination of course. It is a static view of transient being and as such not to be dismissed. So Elizabeth Lennard is no stranger to the instrumentality of creation, an artist of almost wayward originality.

ROY

Sentiment can, and very often does, determine how a model appears to a portraitist, how the model's own sentiment effects the knowledgeable commitment of his appearance, and how the reciprocity of sentiments determines the appearance of a portrait. The portrait, of course, is the durable demonstration of the determinant rapport in sentiment between artist and model, each of whom has offered to it a living element of the self that could not have found expression in any other way but which will survive only briefly, leaving the work of art alone to testify beyond oblivion to the human craving for imperishable sentiment. Portraits inspired by sentiment are naturally not to be likened to those prompted by passion. They suggest, rather, the emotional significance of idealistic, speculative, or sympathetic feelings, which do not entail the blinding exaltation of love. Exemplary illustrations of portraits animated by sentiment are those of Baldassare Castiglione by Raphael, and of François-Marius Granet by Ingres.

This superficial disquisition on the function of sentiment in portraiture is simply by way of introducing myself to the drawing by Gilles Roy. Though by no means the most accomplished likeness of its model, this portrait is the one in which I see more sentiment than in any other of the thirty-seven reproduced here. Prolonged companionship between artist and model may have helped this effect, but a work of art has a will of its own and by virtue of relative perpetuity can convey feeling which eludes transient human intent.

It is the slight tilt of the head in Gilles's drawing which most expresses pensive sensibility touched by an intimation of wistful conjecture. The eyes seem fixed upon a dubious horizon, beyond which may dwell the eternal dissolution that awaits us all. The mouth is speechless, resigned to the futility of language for any attainment of human redemption. Altogether the model's expression is melancholy, submissive, and resigned. But the artist has graced his image with the lovely aura of compassion, preserving the visible present from the all too definitive future, and infusing his portrait of my imaginable self with the saving animation of sentiment. When art can do that, it is absolute absolution, and that is the summum bonum of creation altogether.

I perceive that I have written less about this artist and his portrait than about any of the others. However, I have no regrets. What I have said, I think, amounts to a great deal more than what I have written.

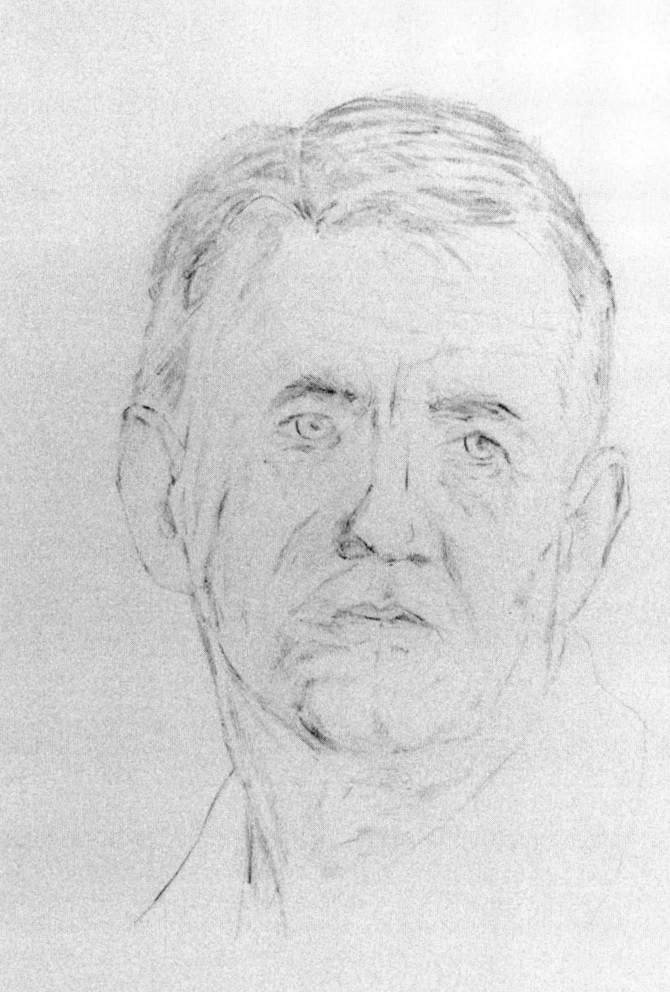

PAPETTI

On June 27, 1994, a Monday, I was in Milan to attend a symposium on Picasso. Afterwards there was a reception and dinner. Because I speak nearly no Italian I found few people to talk to. One of them, however, who had read some of my writing on Alberto and spoke French, was eager to converse with me. Named Alessandro Papetti, he was a small young man attired entirely in black, with black hair and brilliant black eyes. As it happened, he said, he was a painter and also a dedicated admirer of Giacometti. In some catalogues or books he had seen a reproduction of Alberto's painting of me. He modestly but emphatically exclaimed that he, too, would be glad to have a chance to paint me. It seemed to me then, aged over seventy, that I had been posing for portraits off and on for most of my life, and that the time had come to stop. So I thanked him for his offer but observed that as I lived in Paris, it would be impossible for me to pose for an artist resident in Milan. Oh, but that would present no difficulty, Papetti protested, because he could very well work from photographs made by himself, if I were willing, at least, to pose for those during one of his occasional visits to Paris. That request was difficult to refuse, especially as I thought there was little probability that an evening's conversation would produce a painting. Still, I gave my address and telephone number.

So my surprise was considerable sixteen months later when I received a call from the Milanese artist. Temporarily in Paris, he wanted to come to my apartment to take photographs of me preliminary to painting my portrait. I was pleased to see the young man again, enjoying the vivacity and intelligence of his conversation. On a Saturday afternoon, November 4, 1995, he spent an hour snapping photos of me seated in various places in the apartment. They would do very well, he said, departing with rather effusive thanks, leaving me once more with the premonition that I would never see a portrait. When a year or more had passed, I'd rather forgotten about Signor Papetti. Then a package arrived, bringing the catalogue of an exhibition in Italy and a number of photographs, including one in color of my portrait. Dated 1995, it must have been executed immediately after the photographs of the model were made. I was astounded and impressed. But the package, of course, also brought the inevitable request: that I write a preface for the catalogue of an exhibition of recent work—including my portrait!—to take place in November of 1998 in an important gallery in Paris. As usual, I felt it difficult to refuse, though by now I've started to do so. I found the text fairly easy to write, because Papetti's work provides plenty to talk about, and of my many prefaces this is one by which I'm least embarrassed.

The first, and perhaps the most illuminating, thing to be said about the art of Alessandro Papetti is that it is profoundly Italian. It is not his subject matter that evokes the homeland. In this he is truly international, and entirely of his own era despite seeming

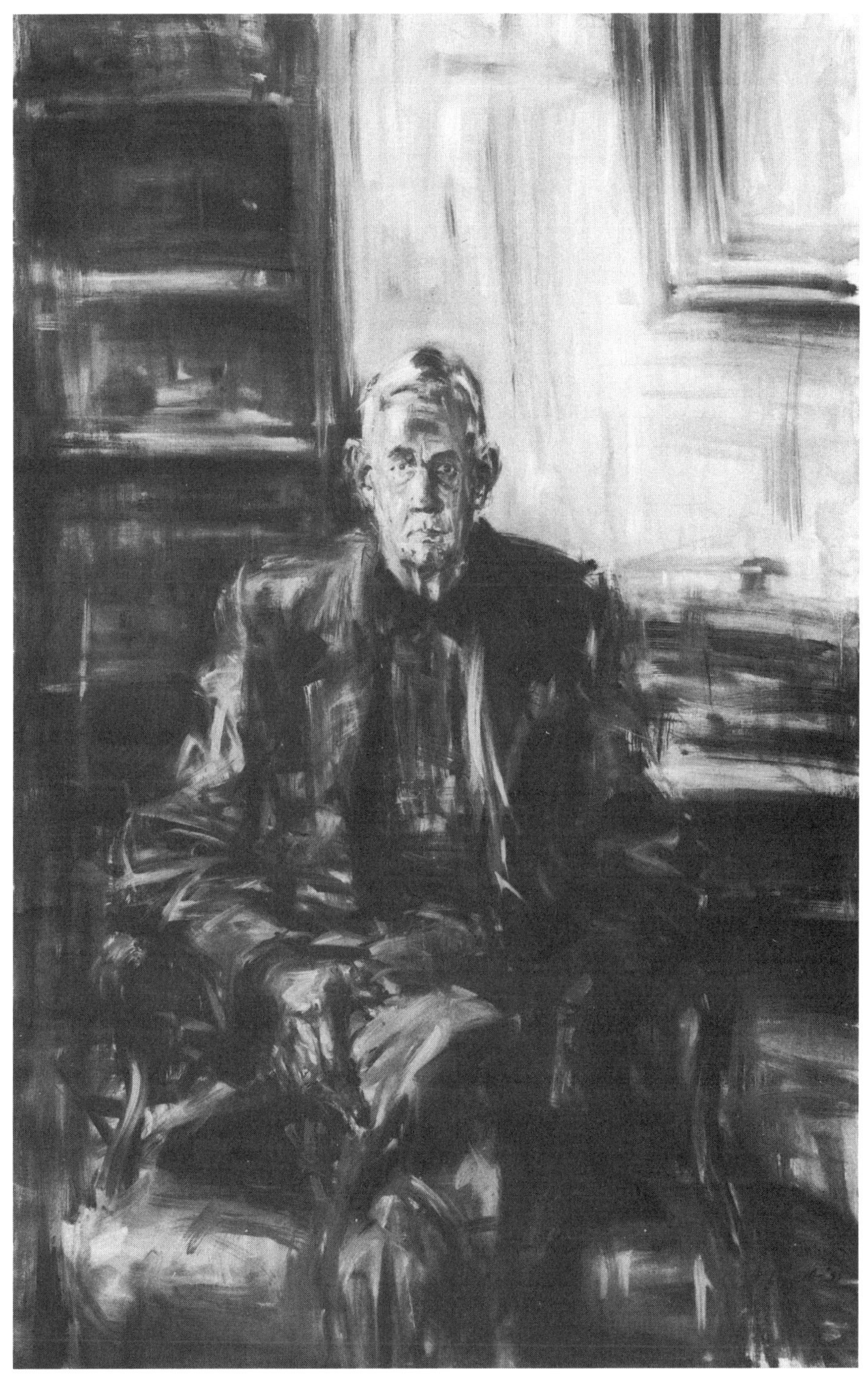

reminiscences of styles of the past. Consider the dizzying representational brushwork. Nowhere north of the Alps has there ever been anything quite like it. One is put in mind of Boldini. Yes, but Papetti does not work with such virtuosity for the sake of fashionable effect. Italianate also is the artist's obsessive focus on space, leading one to think of the first painter to demonstrate the power of art to create a self-contained and self-sustaining universe: Tintoretto. The frenetic movement, ghostly perspective, and supernatural sense of space so characteristic of the Venetian master have plainly made a mark on the vision of the young Milanese artist without, however, overpowering a personal view. In short, he has invented the configuration of an inner world, an achievement essential to the transfiguration that endows with talismanic permanence the transitory detritus of our perishable environment. Papetti's inner world may not be one where we yearn to dwell, but it asserts with crucial authority its right to a place in the artistic universe.

The exhibition opened on a Saturday, the fourteenth of November, 1998, and I went in mid-afternoon to the gallery to have a look at my portrait for the first time. A photograph had not been adequate preparation. The initial reaction was shock. The picture was life-size, but only in size did it appear to bring to life an image of living actuality. Quite simply I felt overwhelmed by the mercurial bravura of the brushwork, which seemed an inextricable turmoil of disorder, the artist himself alien to the violence of his creativity. It was all dashed off in silken grays and blacks amid spatial values appearing to have run riot. This is to say that my first impression was of a disconcerting and somewhat disagreeable power. Then there was my head. The likeness was also surprising. I looked very much present as a recognizable model, but actually as an artistic invention rather than an objective presence. The eyes seem fixed upon the invention, staring rather than gazing, as if confronted by the phantom of a person I might have been in an arbitrary, artificial incarnation. Alarm appears to have seized my features, because the phenomenon before me had become the ghost of a model made believable by the frenzy of the artist, and the hand upon the thigh but a specimen floating in the dubious preservative of paint. All in all, it is not a picture that's easy to turn away from. At the same time, though, it is definitely one that would be difficult to live with.

The exhibition was a critical and commercial success. Half of the paintings were figure studies, nine in all, but none, I thought, as haunting and troubling as the one of me. It demands to be seen in its life-size impetuosity and agitation to be believed, and then that tantalizing question of aesthetic belief will receive a very ambiguous answer.

PALLISER

This final portrait in a series unwittingly initiated fifty-seven years ago was conceived to be the last and executed well after I had already written about the first. I have a friend in the art business to whom I confessed with embarrassment some time ago what eccentric work had been occupying me for almost a year. He insisted that despite my misgivings the project sounded worth pursuing and suggested that an English painter living in Paris, a friend of his and an excellent painter of portraits, produce one for the series. Again I was reluctant to pose, having exhausted by age seventy-eight the vitality needed to commit my appearance to the severe scrutiny of an artist's compulsion. But the suggestion was insistent, accompanied by an invitation to dinner at the painter's apartment in the rue du Bac, where I saw samples of his work. His name was Anthony Palliser. The portraits were skillful, sensitive, traditional, and appeared to be faithful likenesses. I thought that such a portrait might constitute a far more fitting conclusion to the series than Papetti's overwrought image, because the accurate representation of a man inhabiting the shabby suburbs of old age could hardly be condemned as evidence of narcissism. Still, the wonderful ordeal of being a model once again was intimidating. It came out, though, that Mr. Palliser, like Papetti, worked readily, even preferably, from photographs, and was eager to portray me. I can't think why. He proved, in any case, to be an exceptionally companionable and good-natured man. He came to the apartment and made a number of photographs. On Thursday, March 8th, 2001, a large exhibition of Palliser's work was inaugurated at a fashionable gallery in the Faubourg Saint-Honoré. My portrait was one of the dozen or more on exhibition, along with a number of somewhat somber paintings of lonely figures seen from below on dark hillsides silhouetted against vast skies. The portraits, being fine likenesses, were sensitive and vivacious.

Mine was what I had wanted. It was, without mistake, the truthful image of a face I knew only too well. However, I cannot honestly say that I "like" this portrait. It stares too frankly from the far side of Cocteau's mirror, and few people enjoy seeing how their features are disfigured by the physical preparation for oblivion. At the same time, my interest in the image is lively and sincere, because it conveys both human and aesthetic reality with sensuous distinction. The gaze is immediately accurate, communicating thought and feeling imbued—as I see it—with a tolerant and submissive fatalism. Or is it harsh and devious arrogance? The model who searches the artist's creation for the unfathomable secret of the self is toying with inner peril. Palliser's portrait is a penetrating glance at the heart of that secret. As such it poses art's metaphysical conundrum. This supposes that the memory of mankind may be led by art to take kindly to a ludicrous love for imaginative immortality. Such senseless craving for any sort of survival beyond life's normal conclusion unites

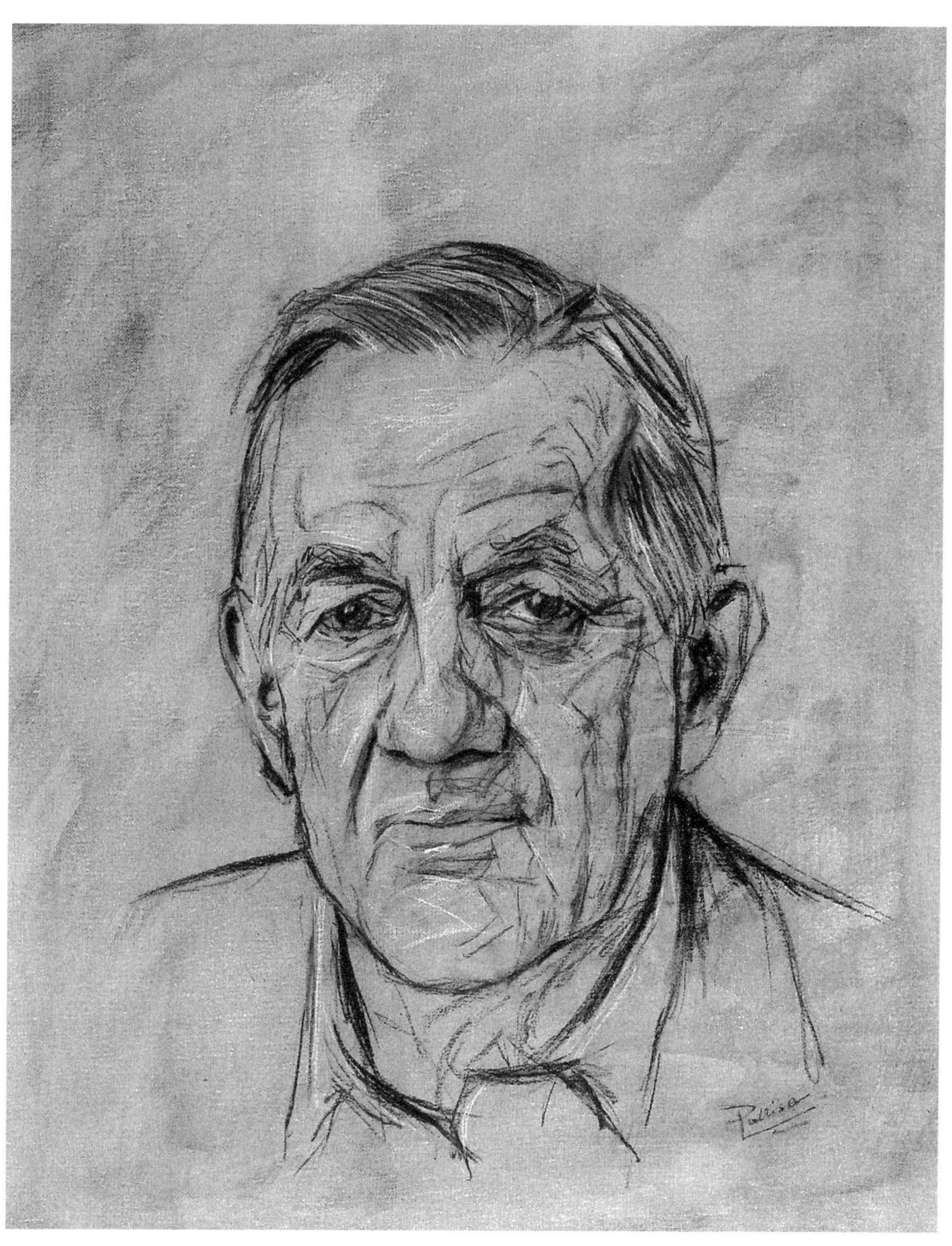

artist and model in a paradoxical semblance of reality which is the basic purpose of a portrait.

And so, though I may not "like" Anthony's portrait, I am pleased by it, for it is more than an accurate and telling likeness. It is a fitting and uncompromising culmination to the unpredictable—the unashamed!—gamble against death begun before I knew it was no game on that day when Picasso first picked up a pencil to make my portrait.

APPENDIX: CATALOGUE OF ILLUSTRATIONS

INDEX

APPENDIX: CATALOGUE OF ILLUSTRATIONS

PABLO PICASSO (1881–1973)

5 Drawing No. 1, pencil on tan paper, 12 × $9\frac{3}{8}$ inches (30.5 × 23.8 cm), signed and dated "Paris, 7 December 1944," inscribed "For James Lord."

11 Drawing No. 2, pencil on cream paper, $19\frac{7}{8}$ × $12\frac{9}{16}$ inches (50.5 × 32 cm), signed and dated "Paris, 27 March 1945," inscribed "For Lord."

YOULA CHAPOVAL (1920–1952)

21 Drawing No. 1, gouache on white paper, $18\frac{1}{2}$ × $12\frac{1}{4}$ inches (47 × 31.1 cm), signed and dated "4 October 1945," inscribed "For Lord, his friend."

25 Drawing No. 2, gouache on white paper, $18\frac{1}{2}$ × $12\frac{1}{4}$ inches (47 × 31.1 cm), signed and dated "4 October 1945," inscribed "for James Poet."

ROGER GINDERTAEL (dates unknown)

29 Drawing in charcoal on white paper, 25 × $18\frac{1}{2}$ inches (63.5 × 47 cm), signed and dated "45."

PAUL MONDAIN (dates unknown)

35 Charcoal drawing on cream paper, 21 × $18\frac{1}{2}$ inches (53.5 × 44.5 cm), unsigned, undated, executed in 1945.

39 Oil painting on canvas, $19\frac{3}{4}$ × $18\frac{1}{2}$ inches (50.2 × 47 cm), unsigned, dated "Paris 49."

THEOPHILUS BROWN (b. 1919)

47 Pencil drawing on white paper, $21\frac{1}{2}$ × $15\frac{1}{2}$ inches (54.6 × 39.4 cm), unsigned, dated "Paris 49."

LUCIAN FREUD (b. 1922)

51 Black-and-white chalk drawing on brown paper, 13 × $19\frac{1}{4}$ inches (33 × 23.5 cm), unsigned, undated, executed in 1950.

JEAN COCTEAU (1889–1963)

59 Pencil drawing on white paper, $13\frac{1}{2}$ × 10 inches (34.3 × 25.4 cm), signed, dated "Santo Sospir, August 1951," inscribed "to James, his friend Jean."

DORA MAAR (1907–1997)

65 Photograph, $9\frac{3}{8}$ × 7 inches (23.8 × 17.8 cm), unsigned, undated, executed in 1957.

69 Pencil drawing on white paper, $19\frac{3}{4}$ × $13\frac{1}{4}$ inches (50.2 × 33.7 cm), unsigned, undated, executed in 1954, bearing the stamp of the posthumous auction sale of Dora Maar's possessions, "DM 1998."

JOHN CRAXTON (b. 1922)

75 Black-and-white chalk on blue-gray paper, 17 × 12 inches (43.2 × 30.5 cm), signed and dated, "Paris October 1954," inscribed "To James."

ALBERTO GIACOMETTI (1901–1966)

81 Drawing No. 1, pencil on cream paper, $19\frac{3}{4}$ × $12\frac{3}{4}$ inches (50.2 × 32.4 cm), signed and dated "1954."

85 Drawing No. 2, pencil on cream paper, $19\frac{3}{4}$ × $12\frac{3}{4}$ inches (50.2 × 32.4 cm), signed and dated "1954."

89 Drawing No. 3, pencil on cream paper, $19\frac{3}{4}$ × $12\frac{3}{4}$ inches (50.2 × 32.4 cm), signed and dated "1954."

93 Drawing No. 4, detail; pencil on cream paper, $19\frac{3}{4}$ × $12\frac{3}{4}$ inches (50.2 × 32.4 cm), signed and dated "1954."

97 Oil painting on canvas, 46 × $32\frac{1}{8}$ inches (117 × 81.5 cm), signed and dated "1954."

RANDALL MORGAN (b. 1920)

103 Pencil on white paper, signed, undated, executed in 1957.

BALTHUS (BALTHASAR KLOSSOWSKI; 1908–2001)

109 Drawing No. 1, pencil on cream paper, 15 × $11\frac{3}{8}$ inches (38 × 29 cm), signed "B," dated "1959."

115 Drawing No. 2, pencil on cream paper, 20 × $16\frac{1}{2}$ inches (51 × 42 cm), signed "B," dated "1959."

121 Drawing No. 3, pencil on cream paper, 20 × $16\frac{1}{2}$ inches (51 × 42 cm), signed "B," dated "1959."

RAYMOND MASON (b. 1921)

129 Watercolor on white paper, $16\frac{1}{4} \times 12\frac{3}{4}$ inches (41.3 × 32.5 cm), signed and dated "1972."

HENRI CARTIER-BRESSON (b. 1908)

135 Photograph on white paper, $11\frac{1}{4} \times 7\frac{1}{2}$ inches (28.5 × 19 cm), signed "Henri" and inscribed "For James in friendship." Executed in 1975.

143 Drawing, pencil on white paper, $12 \times 9\frac{1}{2}$ inches (30.5 × 24.1 cm), signed "H.C-B." and dated "July 1978."

SAM SZAFRAN (b. 1934)

151 Drawing No. 1, charcoal on white paper, $30 \times 22\frac{3}{8}$ inches (76.2 × 51 cm), signed, executed in 1972, inscribed "For James Lord."

155 Drawing No. 2, charcoal on white paper, $30 \times 22\frac{3}{8}$ inches (76.2 × 51 cm), signed, executed in 1972.

JEAN-MAX TOUBEAU (b. 1945)

159 Pencil drawing on white paper, $13 \times 9\frac{7}{8}$ inches (33 × 25.2 cm), signed "Jean-Max," dated "19 May 1975," and inscribed "For James in friendship."

IVAN THEIMER (b. 1944)

165 Sculpture in bronze, $9\frac{1}{2} \times 6$ inches (24.1 × 15.2 cm), signed and dated "1985–86, Paris," and numbered "Artist's Proof 1."

ANONYMOUS RUSSIAN ARTIST (dates unknown)

173 Pencil on white paper, $6\frac{5}{8} \times 4\frac{3}{8}$ inches (16.8 × 11.1 cm), signed illegibly and dated "1995."

JEAN-BAPTISTE SÉCHERET (b. 1957)

179 Print No. 1, etching on gray paper, $15\frac{1}{2} \times 14\frac{1}{4}$ inches (39.4 × 36.2 cm), signed "Jean-Baptiste," dated "3 April 1997," marked "first state $\frac{1}{3}$," and inscribed "James, for him, in friendship."

183 Print No. 2, monotype on gray paper, $14\frac{1}{2} \times 11\frac{1}{2}$ inches (36.7 × 29.2 cm), signed and dated "1997," and inscribed "James."

THOMAS CORDELL (b. 1951)

189 Oil on board, $13\frac{3}{4} \times 10\frac{7}{8}$ inches (35 × 27.7 cm), signed, executed in 1995.

ELIZABETH LENNARD (b. 1953)

195 Multiple photographs on white paper painted in blue and gray watercolor, $15\frac{3}{8} \times 12\frac{7}{8}$ inches (39 × 32.7 cm), signed and dated "1997," and inscribed "James Lord."

GILLES ROY (b. 1948)

201 Pencil drawing on white paper, $19 \times 12\frac{3}{4}$ inches (48.2 × 32.4 cm), signed, executed in 1992.

ALESSANDRO PAPETTI (b. 1958)

205 Oil on canvas, $79\frac{3}{4} \times 49$ inches (202.2 × 124.5 cm), signed and dated "1995."

ANTHONY PALLISER (b. 1949)

211 Black-and-white chalk and charcoal on cream paper, 26 × $18\frac{3}{4}$ inches (66 × 47.6 cm), signed, executed in 2000.

INDEX

D

E

F

G

R

S